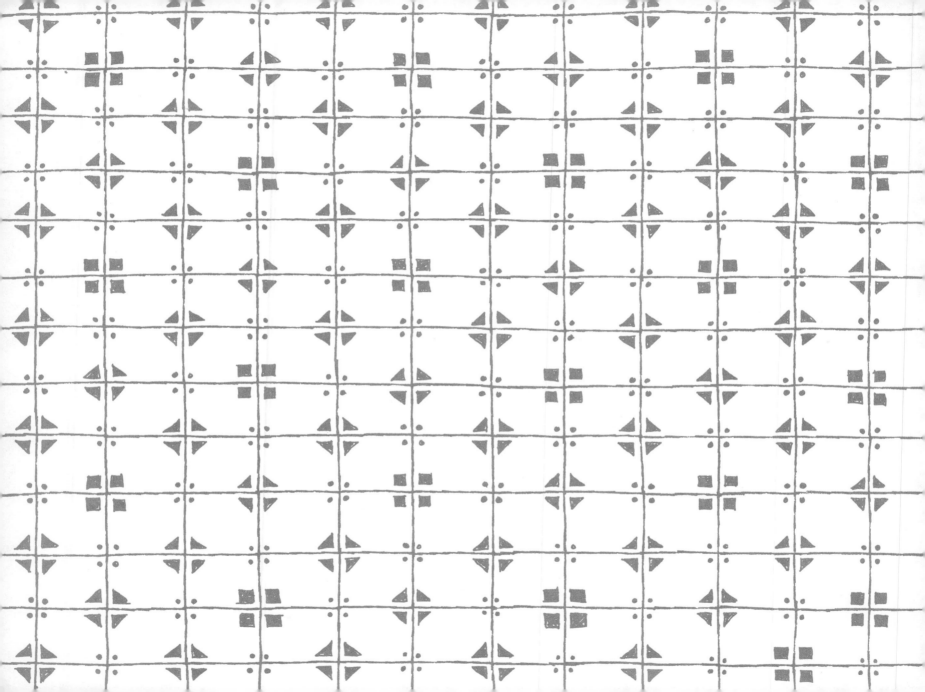

ED EMBERLEY'S BIG ORANGE DRAWING BOOK

LITTLE, BROWN & COMPANY
BOSTON TORONTO

LIBRARY OF CONGRESS
CATALOGING IN PUBLICATION DATA

EMBERLEY, ED.
  ED EMBERLEY'S BIG ORANGE DRAWING BOOK.

  SUMMARY: STEP-BY-STEP INSTRUCTIONS
FOR DRAWING PEOPLE AND ANIMALS USING
A MINIMUM OF LINE AND CIRCLE
COMBINATIONS.
  1. DRAWING--TECHNIQUE--JUVENILE LITERATURE.
2. ORANGE(COLOR) IN ART--JUVENILE LITERATURE.
[1. DRAWING--TECHNIQUE] I.TITLE. II.TITLE:
BIG ORANGE DRAWING BOOK.
NC 655.E45   741.2'4   80-16271
ISBN   0-316-23418-4
ISBN   0-316-23419-2 (PBK.)
HC: 11
PB: 20 19 18 17 16 15 14 13

PUBLISHED SIMULTANEOUSLY IN CANADA BY
LITTLE, BROWN & COMPANY LTD (CANADA)
WOR
PRINTED IN THE UNITED STATES OF AMERICA

IF YOU CAN DRAW THESE SIMPLE SHAPES

(△ ○ □ D · I L ∧ C)

THERE'S A GOOD CHANCE THAT YOU WILL BE ABLE TO DRAW
AT LEAST MOST OF THE THINGS IN THIS BOOK .

STEP-BY-STEP INSTRUCTIONS SHOW YOU HOW.

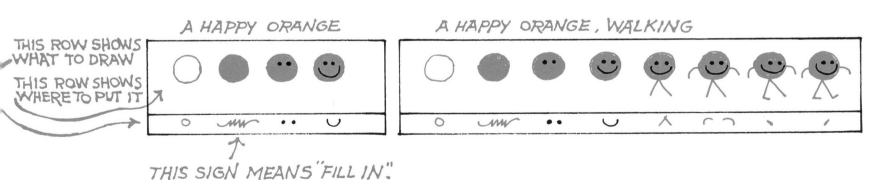

A HAPPY ORANGE

A HAPPY ORANGE , WALKING

THIS ROW SHOWS
WHAT TO DRAW

THIS ROW SHOWS
WHERE TO PUT IT

THIS SIGN MEANS "FILL IN".

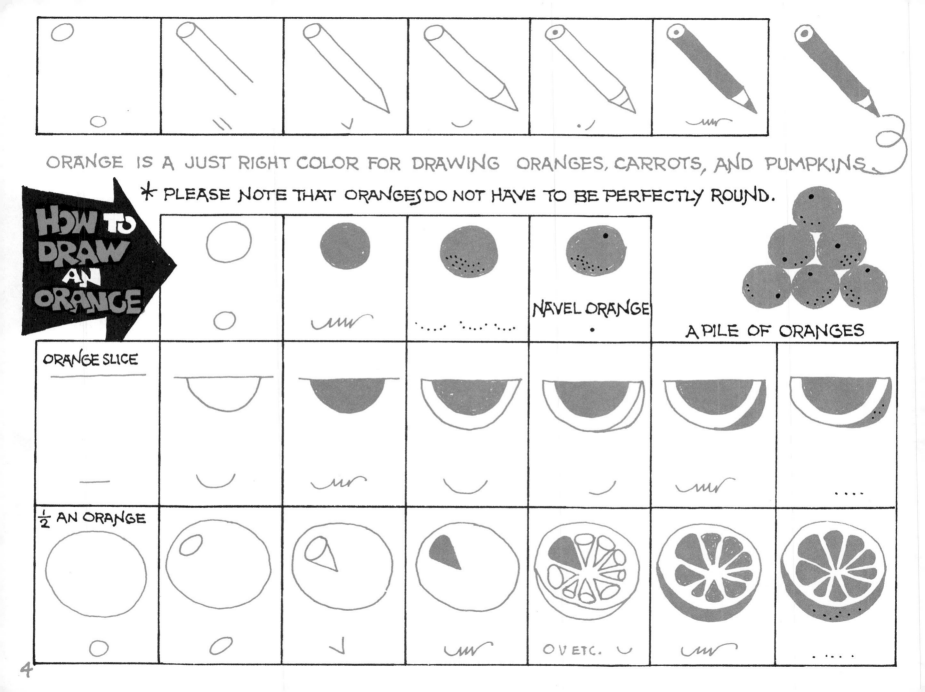

ORANGE IS A JUST RIGHT COLOR FOR DRAWING ORANGES, CARROTS, AND PUMPKINS.

*PLEASE NOTE THAT ORANGES DO NOT HAVE TO BE PERFECTLY ROUND.

HOW TO DRAW AN ORANGE

NAVEL ORANGE

A PILE OF ORANGES

ORANGE SLICE

½ AN ORANGE

OV ETC.

4

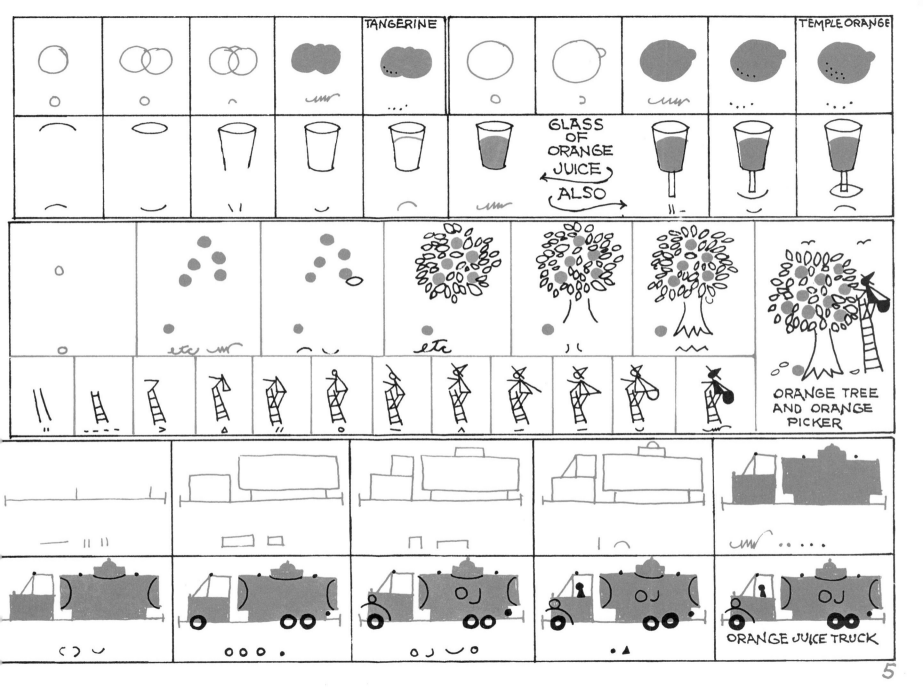

TANGERINE

TEMPLE ORANGE

GLASS
OF
ORANGE
JUICE
ALSO

ORANGE TREE
AND ORANGE
PICKER

ORANGE JUICE TRUCK

5

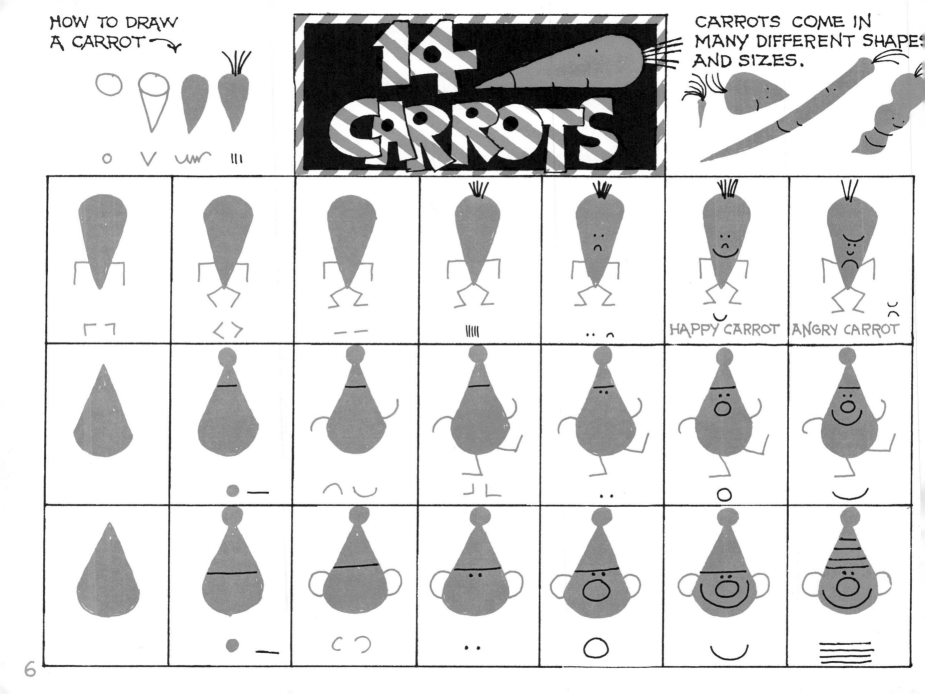

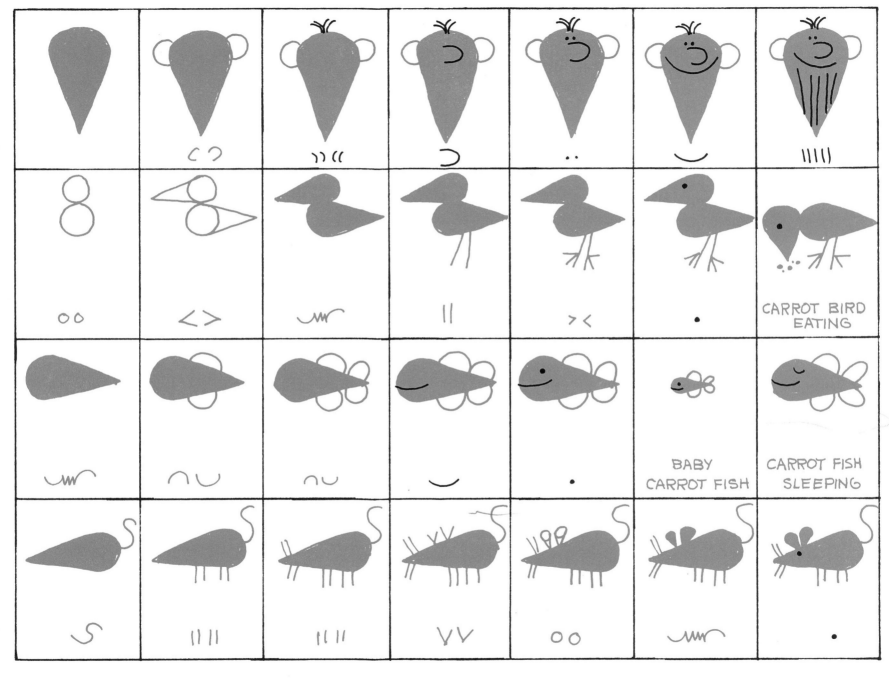

CARROT BIRD
EATING

BABY
CARROT FISH

CARROT FISH
SLEEPING

7

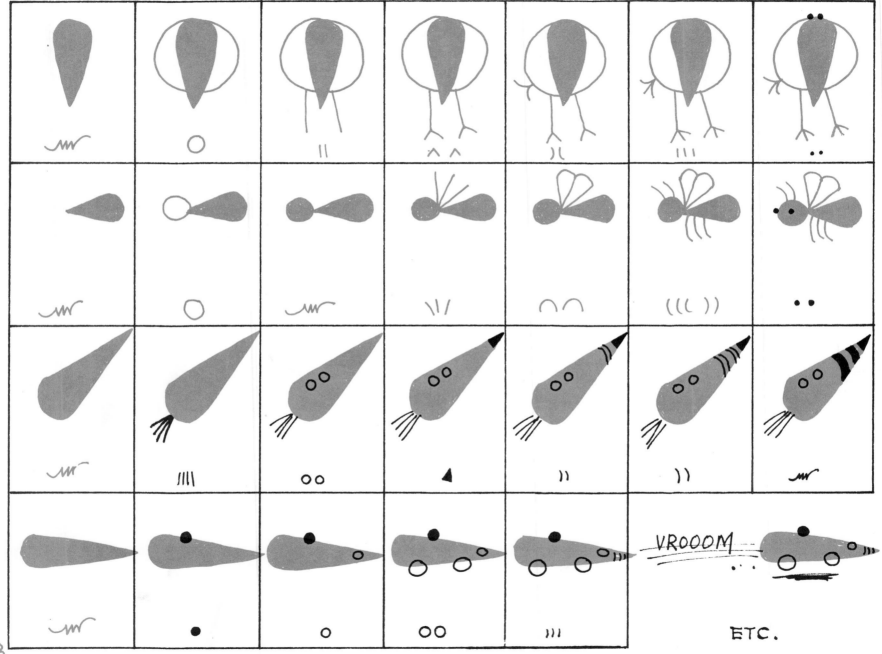

VROOOM

ETC.

8

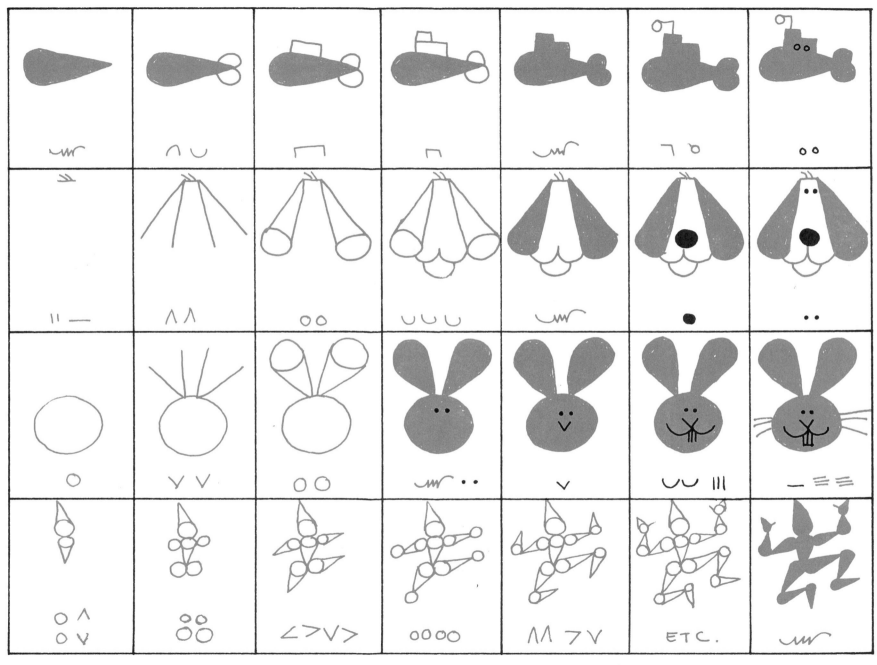

9

PUMPKINS AND JACK O'LANTERNS

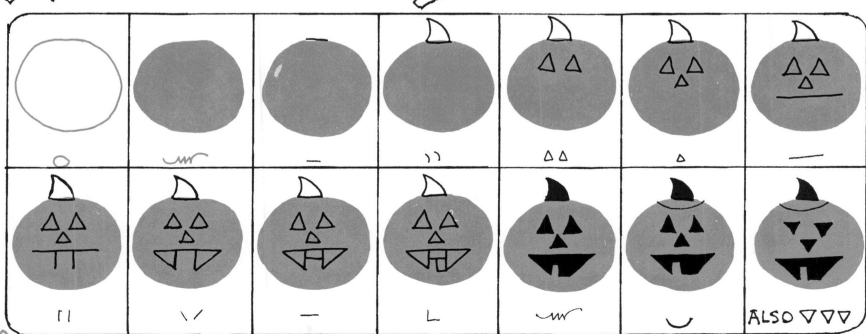

ALSO ▽ ▽▽

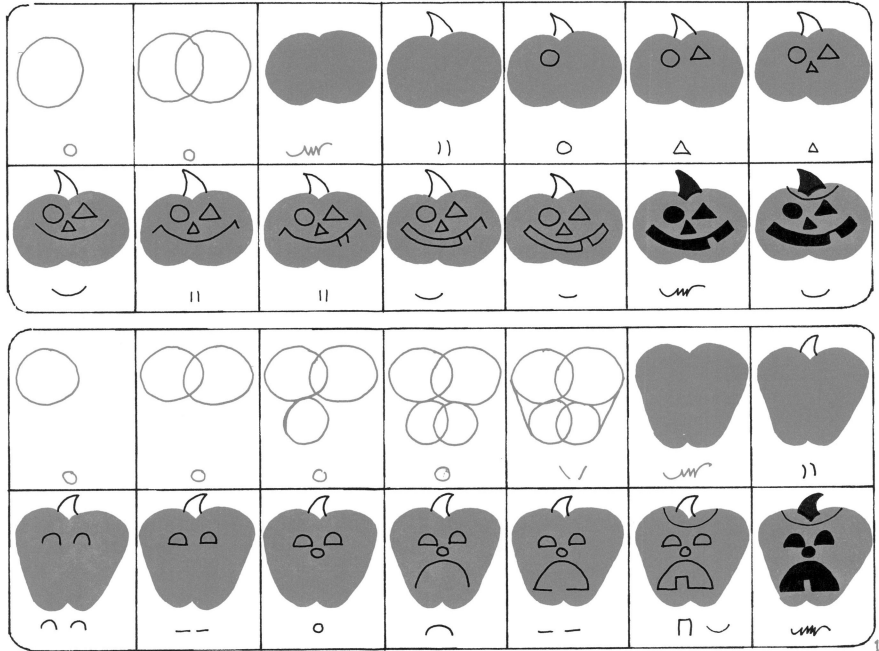

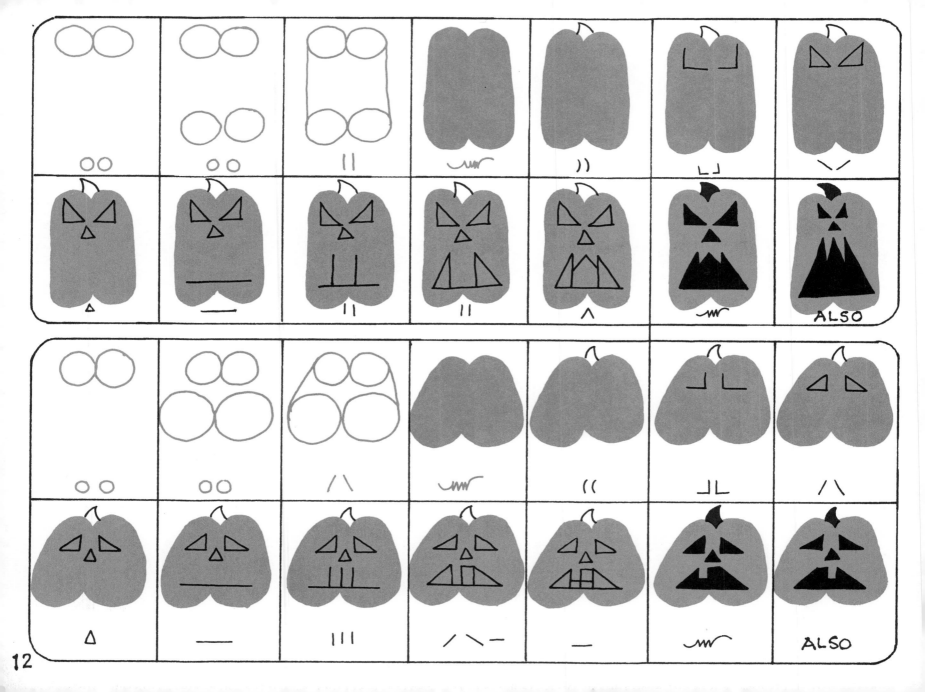

ALSO

ALSO

THIS WAY TO MORE HALLOWEEN STUFF

13

HALLOWEEN SILHOUETTES

15

16

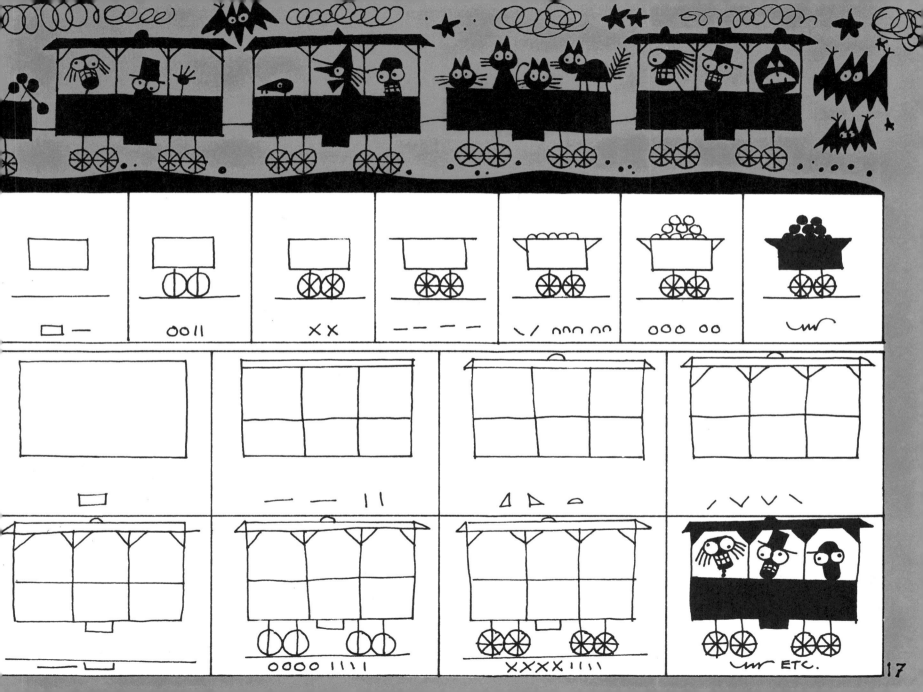

□ —

OO I I

X X

— — — ·

\/ \/ ᴓᴓᴓ ᴓᴓ

OOO OO

ᴗᴡ

□

— — — I I

Δ ▷ ◠

/ \/ \/ \

— □

OOOO I I I I

XXXX I I I I

ᴗᴡ ETC.

17

19

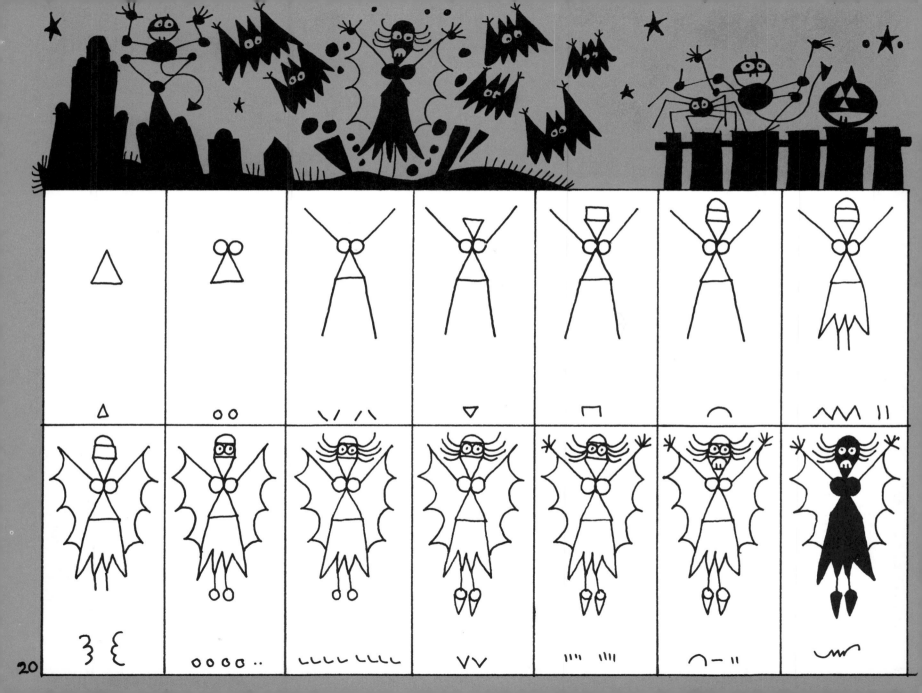

21

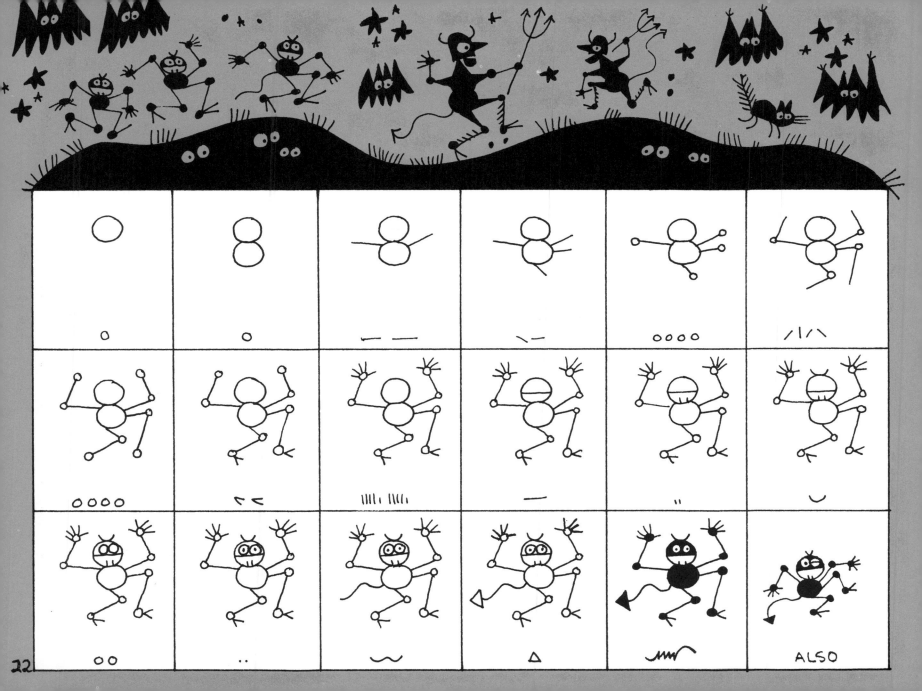

ALSO

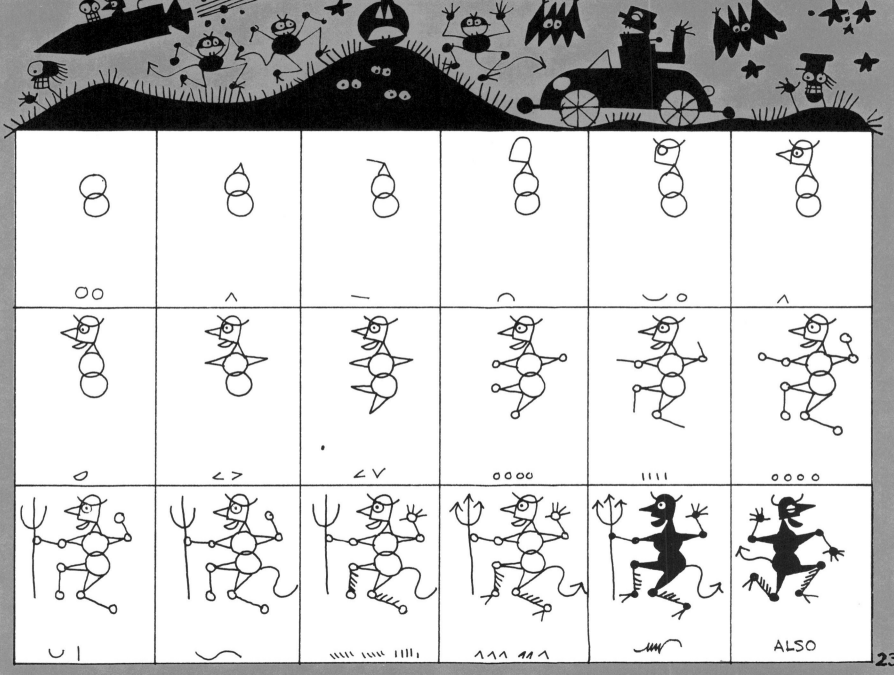

ALSO

23

24

ALSO

26

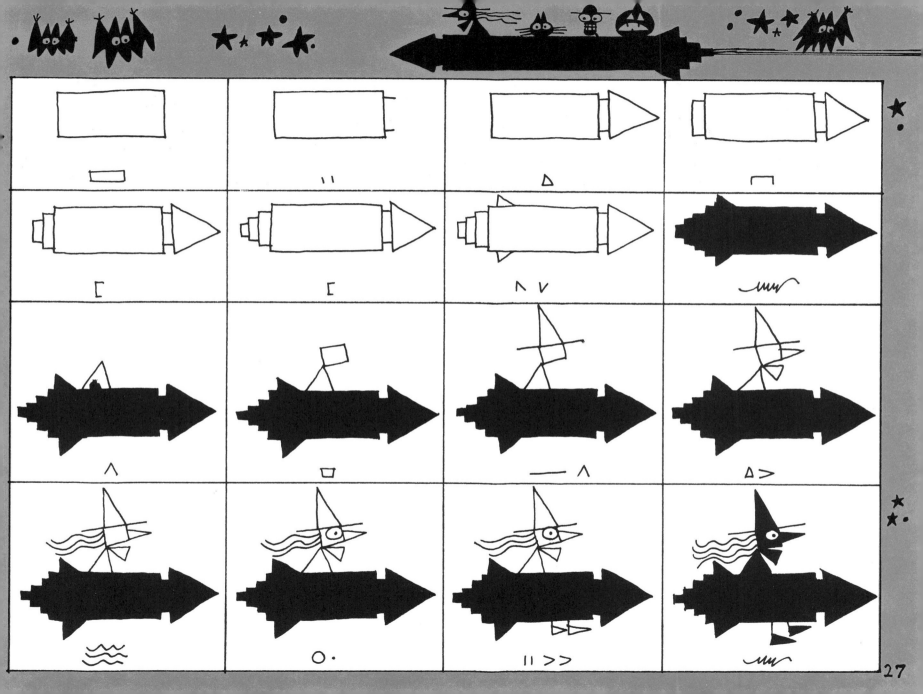

27

28

29

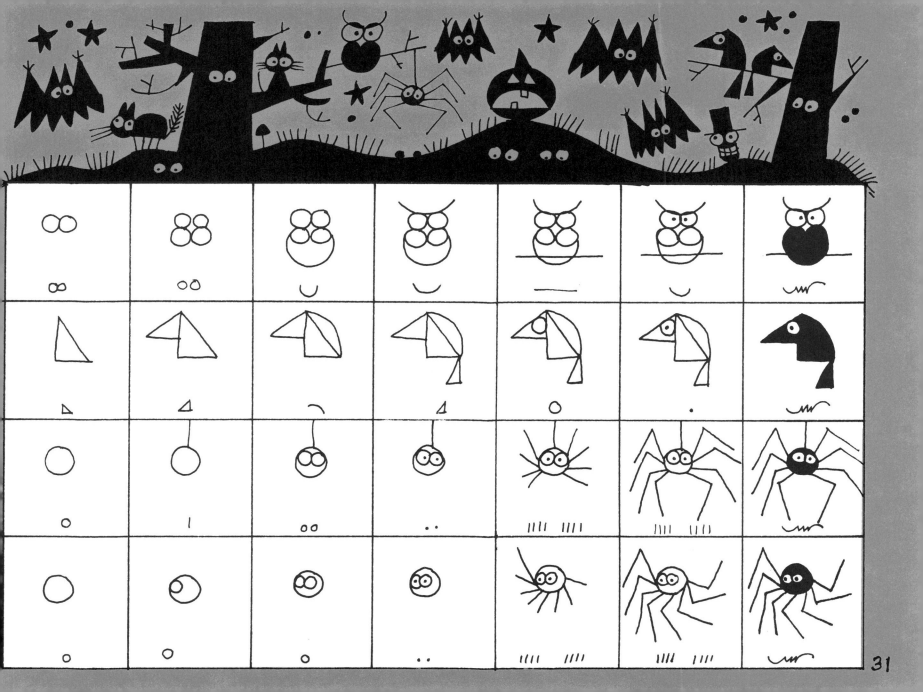

SPOOKY HOUSE

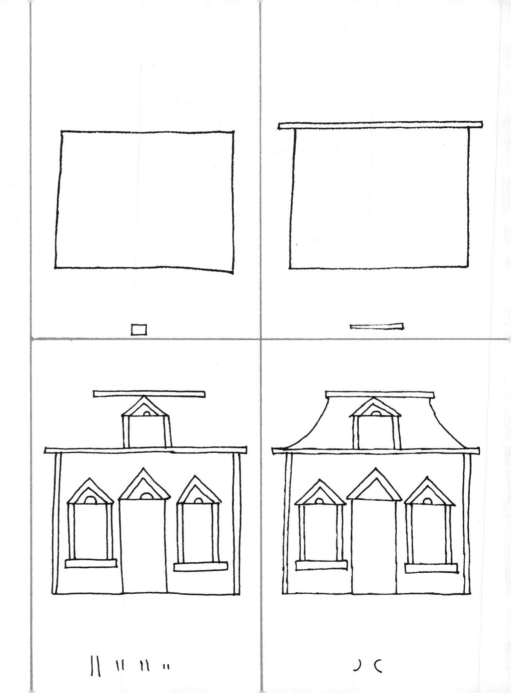

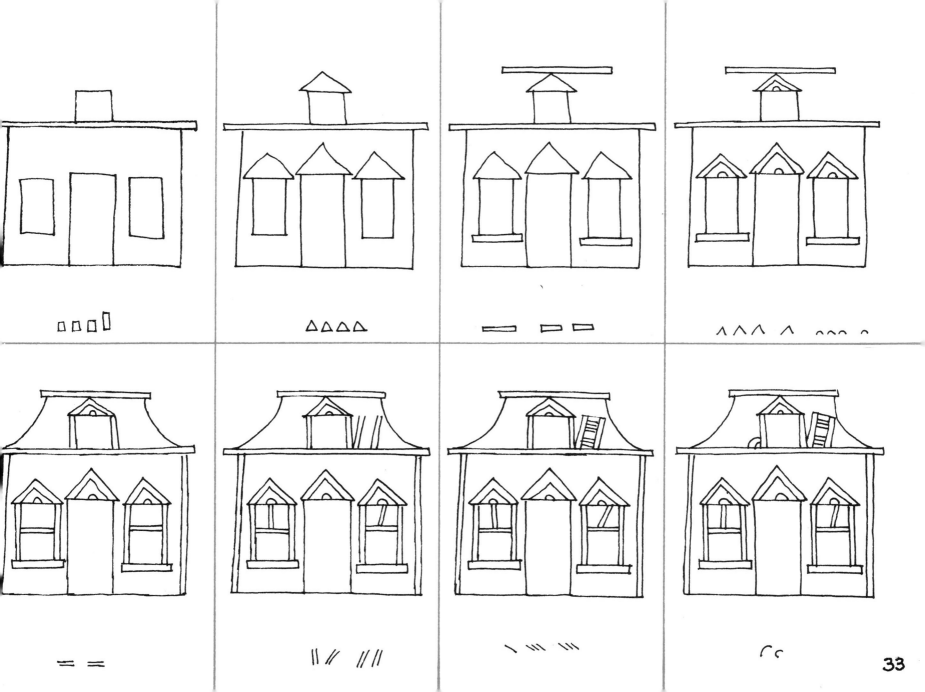

33

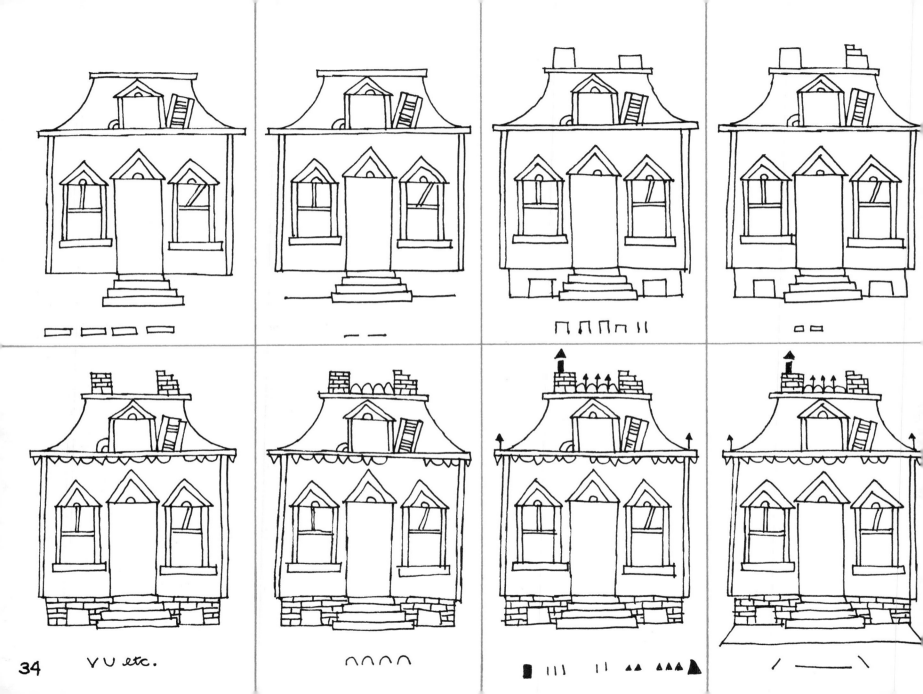

34 VU etc.

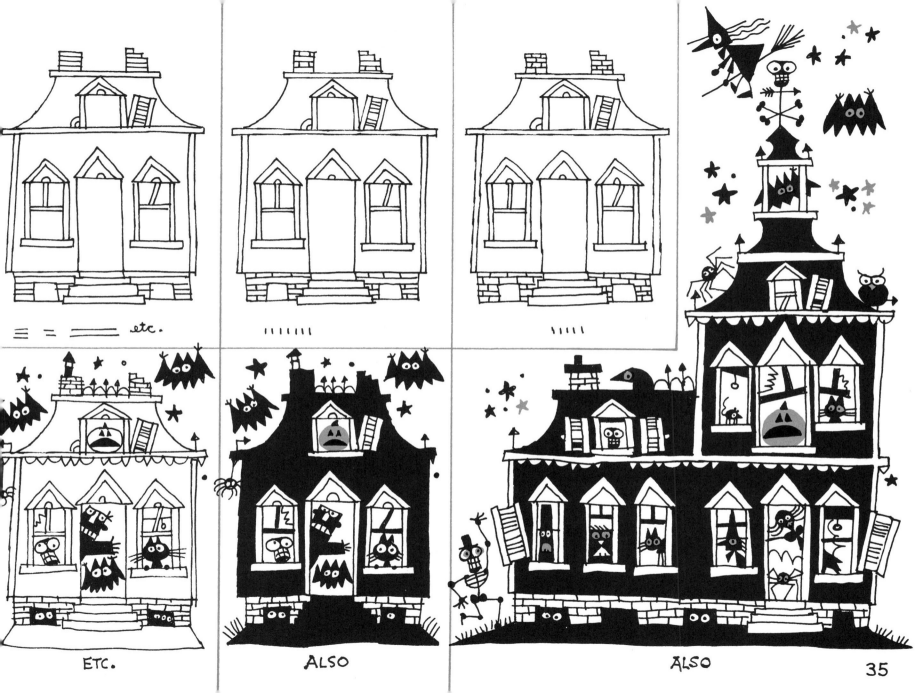

etc.

ETC.

ALSO

ALSO

35

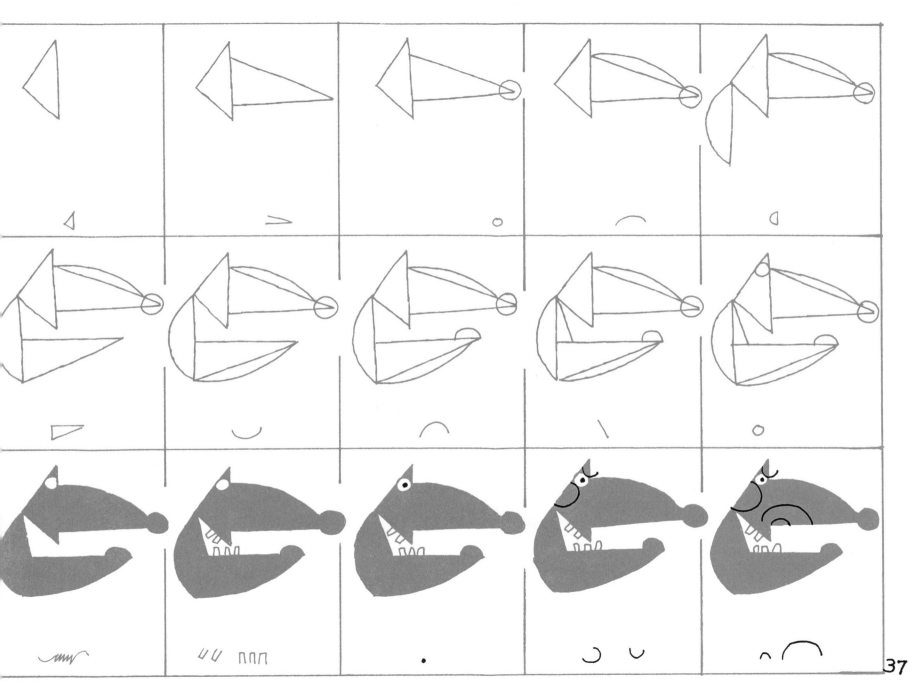

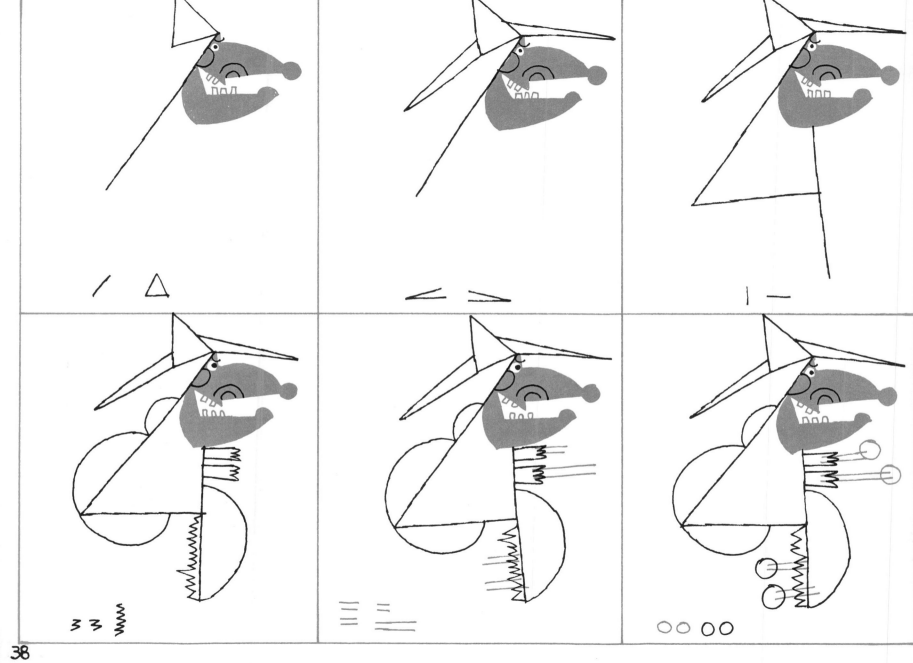

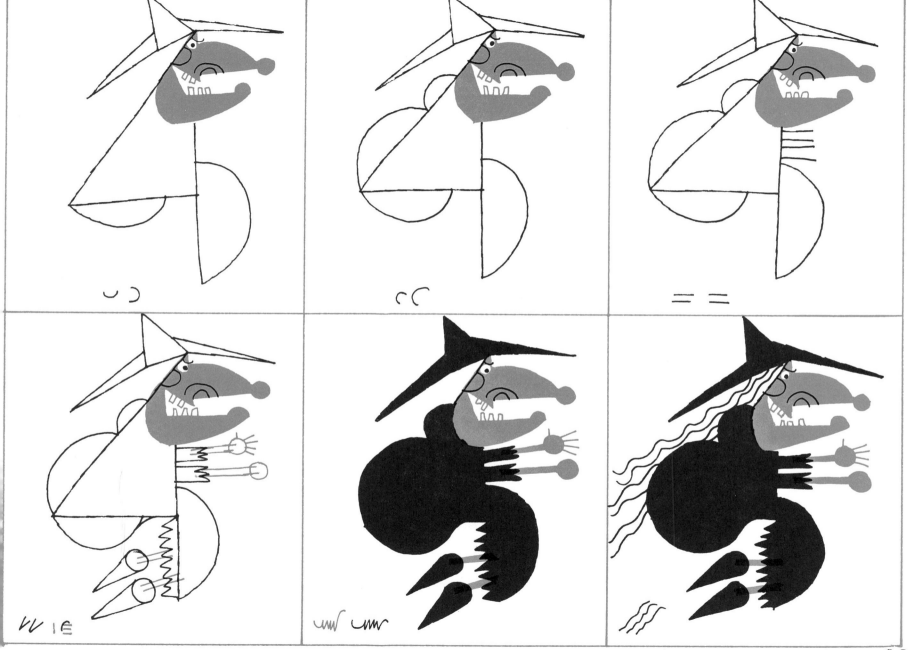

39

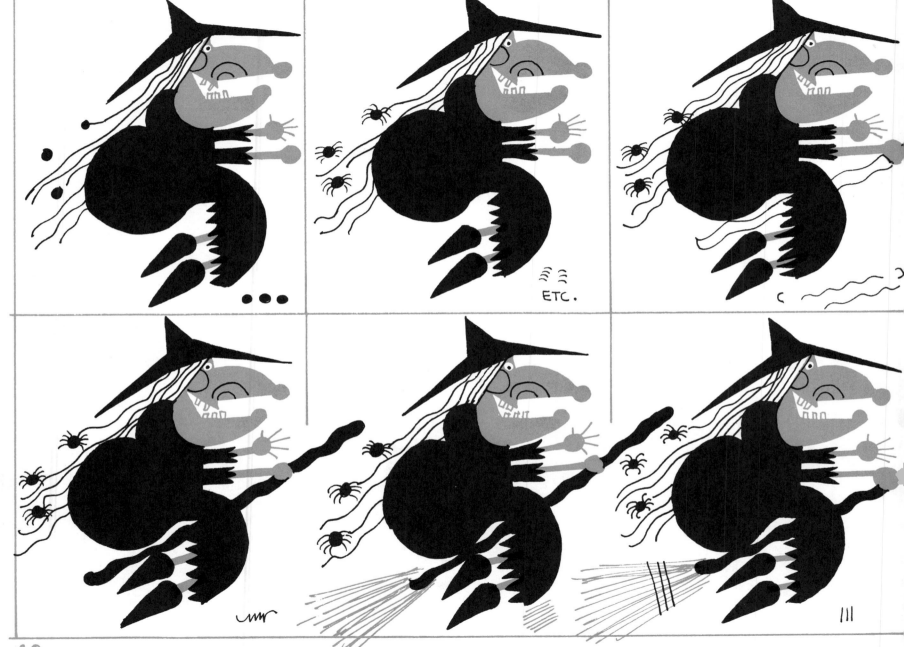

ETC.

40

41

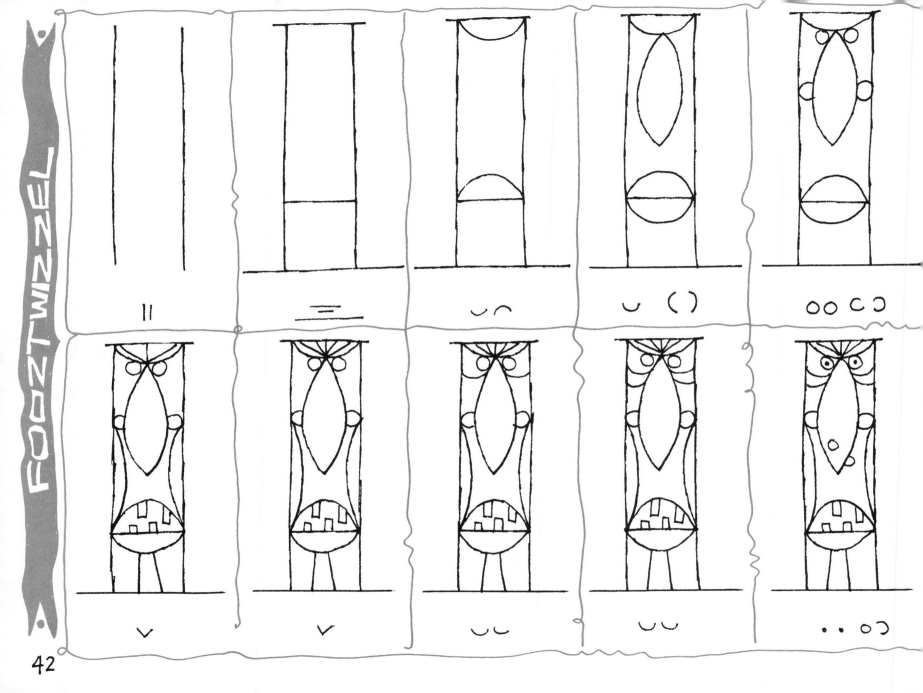

42

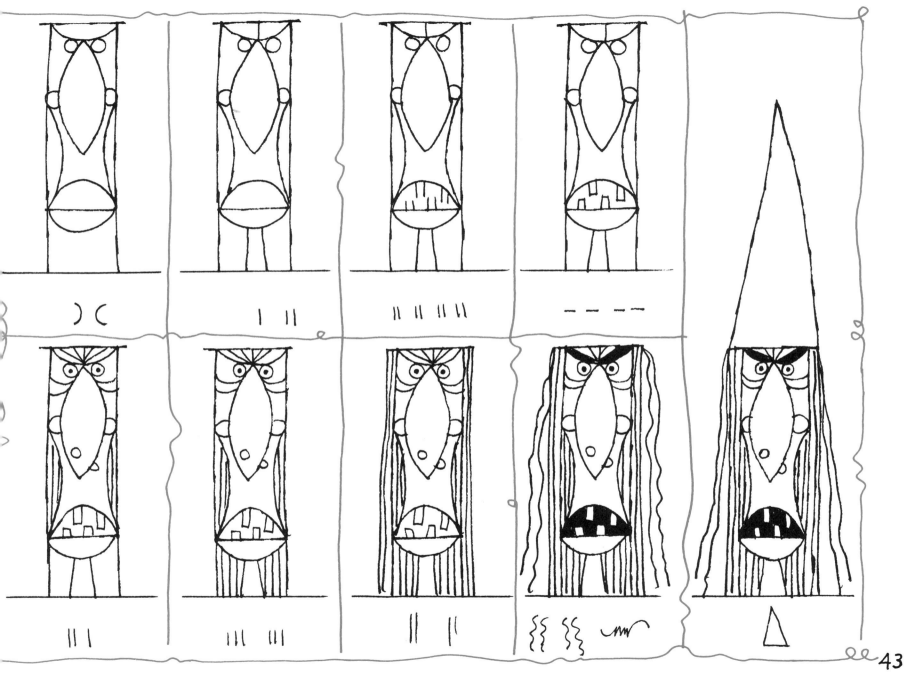

ETC.

44

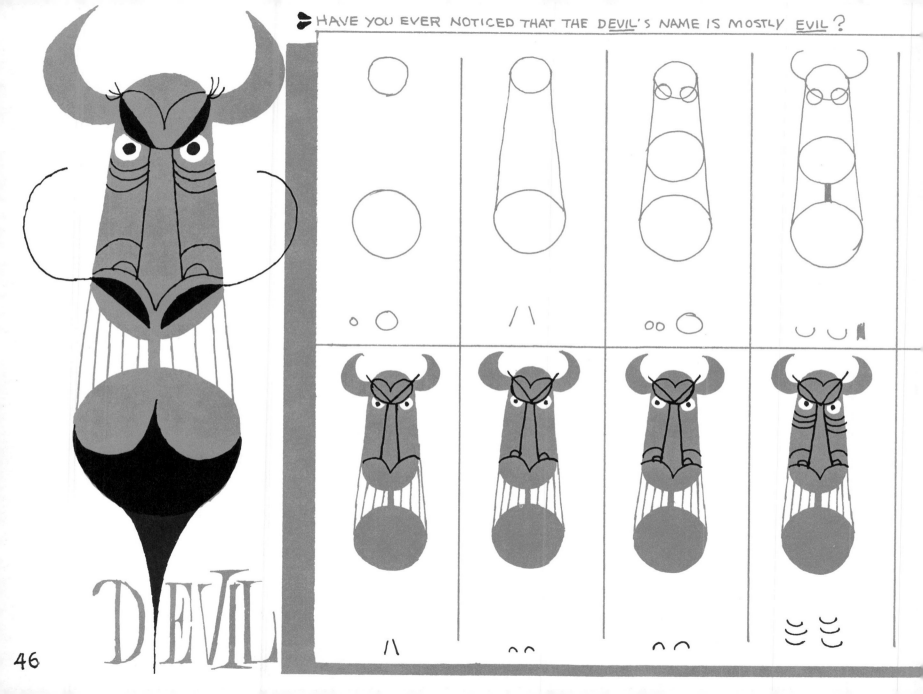

D EVIL

46

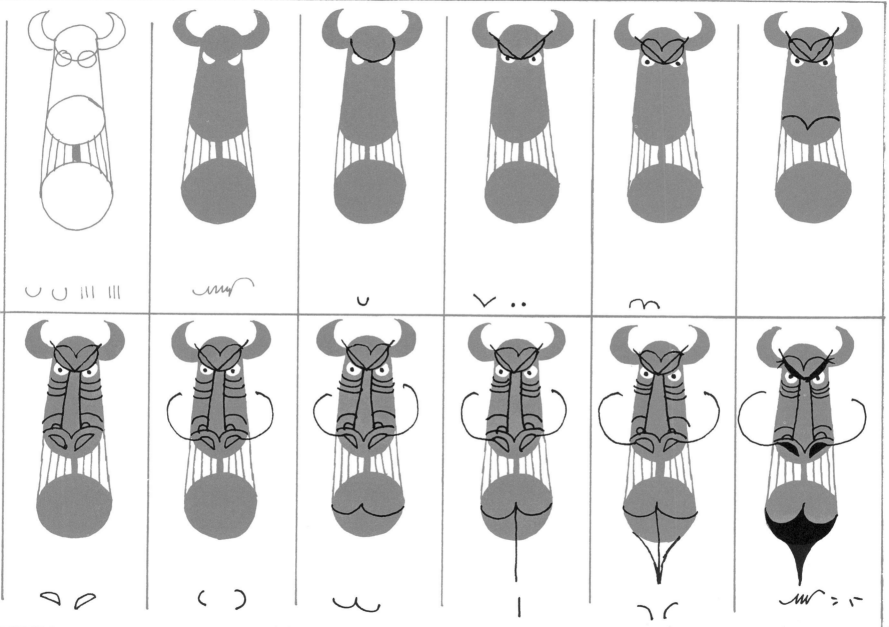

SKULL

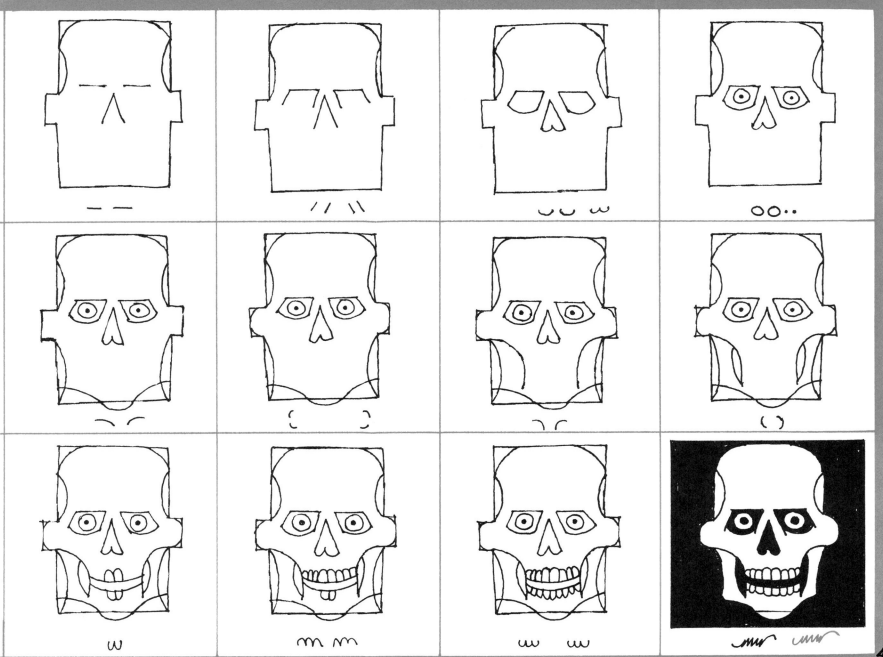

49

O.W.Livingstone

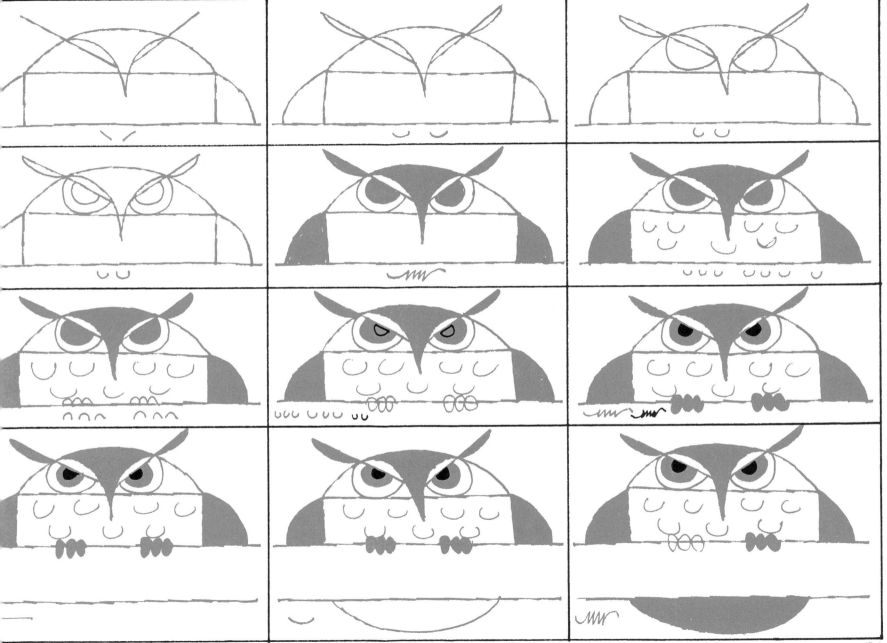

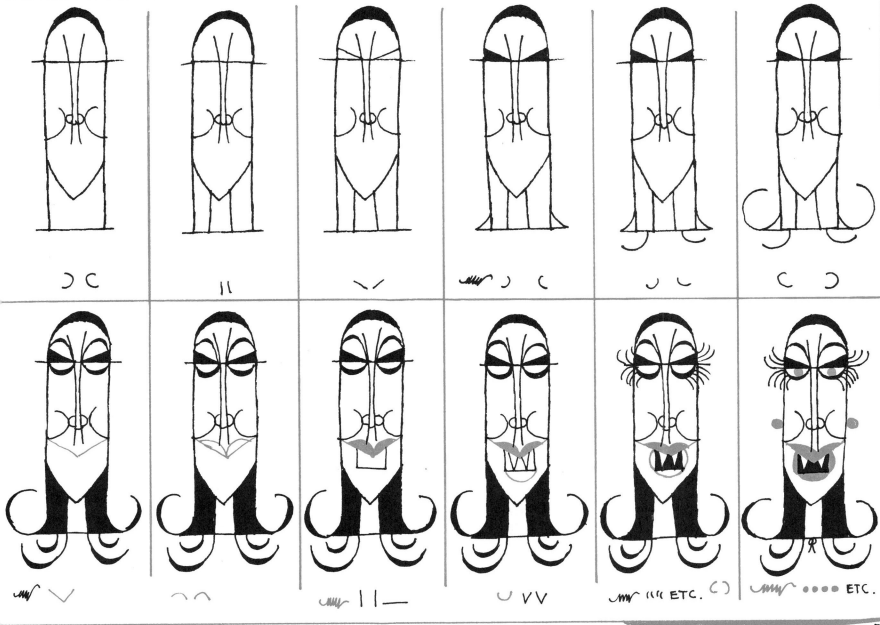

SCHNIDER THE HALLOWEEN SPIDER

ETC

54

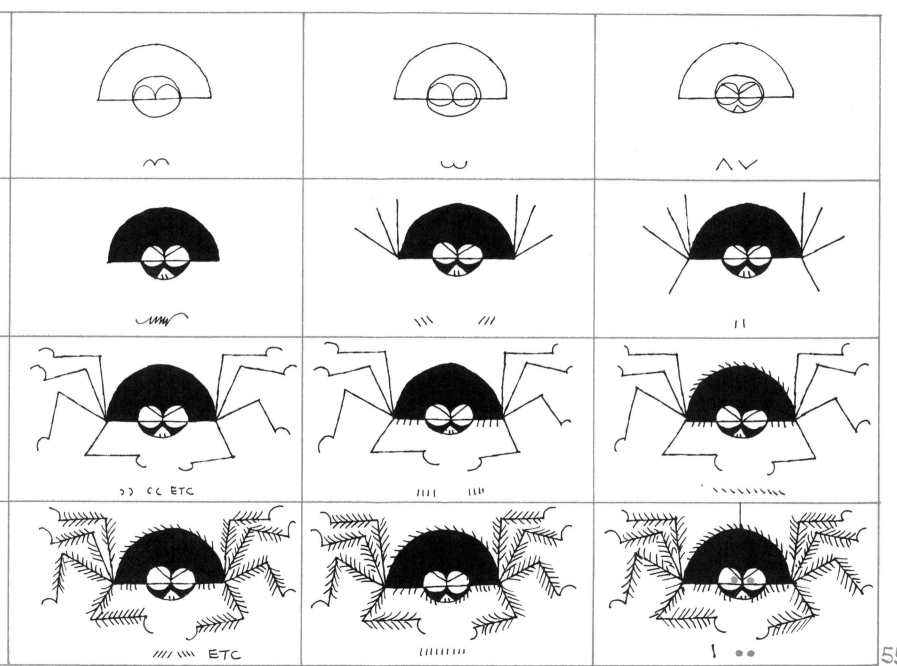

55

OGRE

ETC.

57

MORE HALLOWEEN CATS

58

MEAN MOUTH SHUT EYE SHUT EYES SHUT BACK VIEW

MEOWWW

59

BUTTERCUP

60

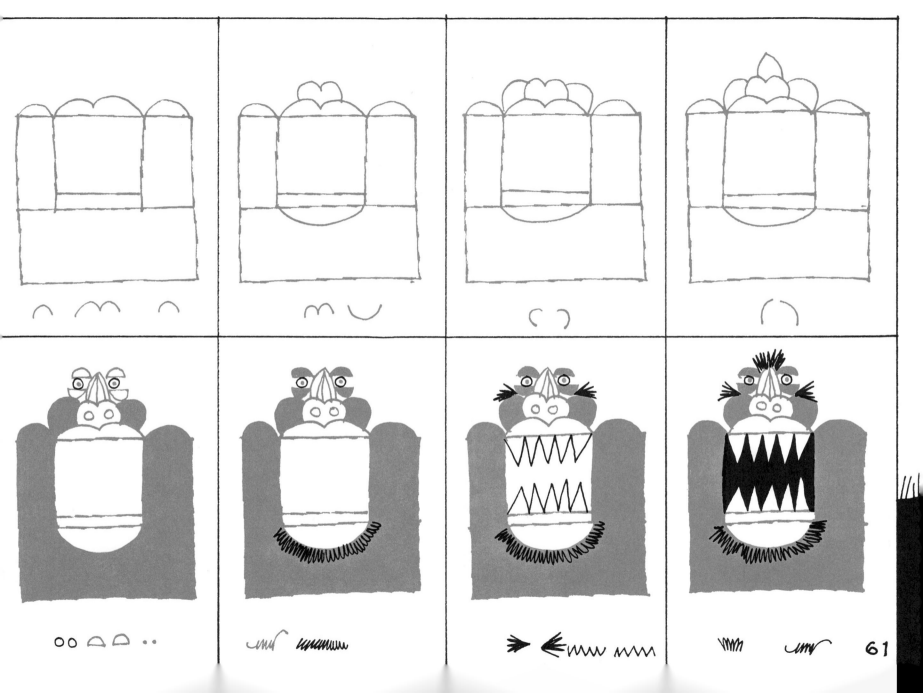

61

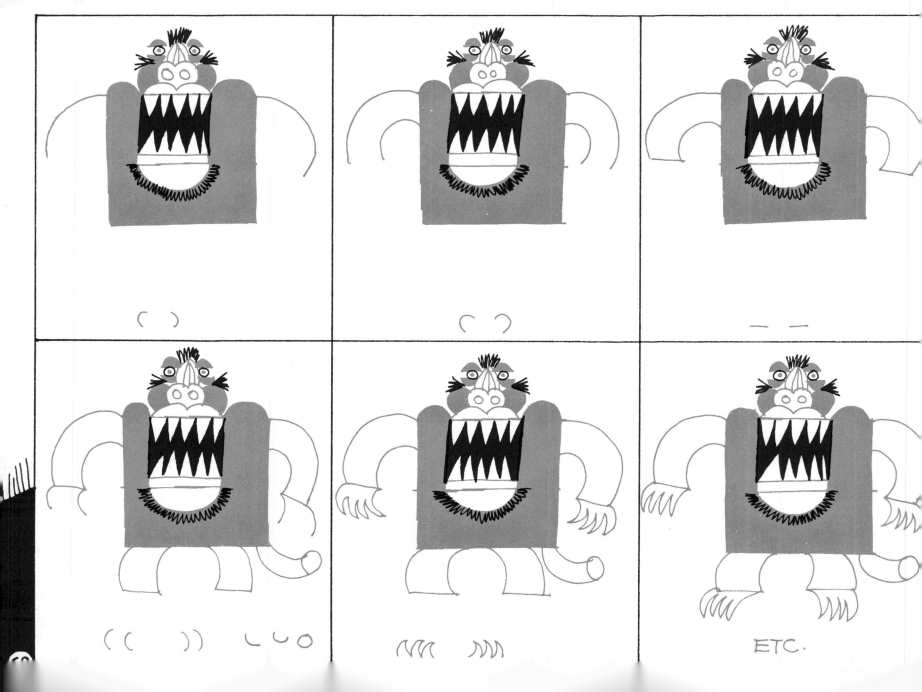

ETC.

ETC.

tiger cub

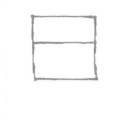

〓	〜

etc.

65

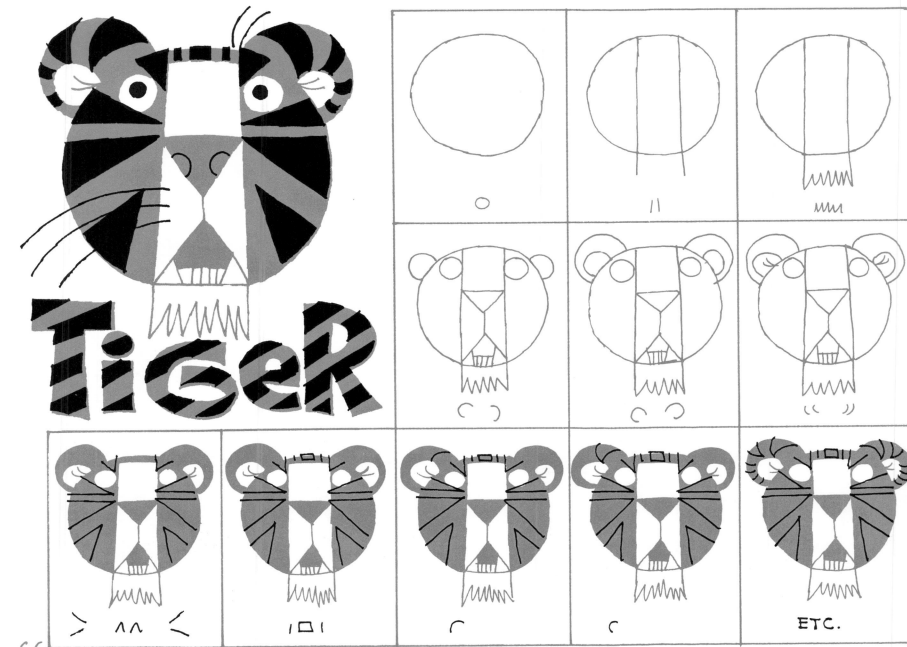

Tiger

ETC.

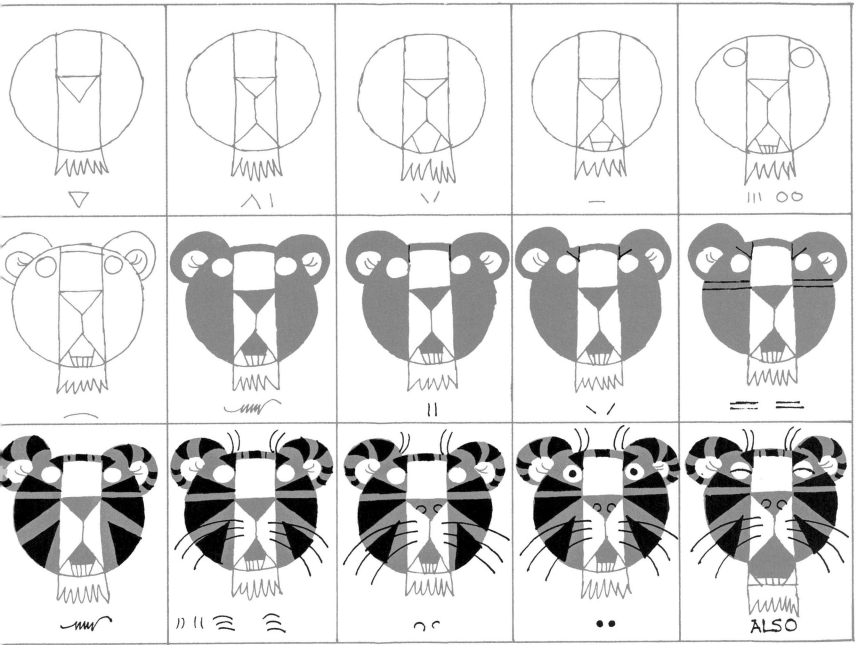

67

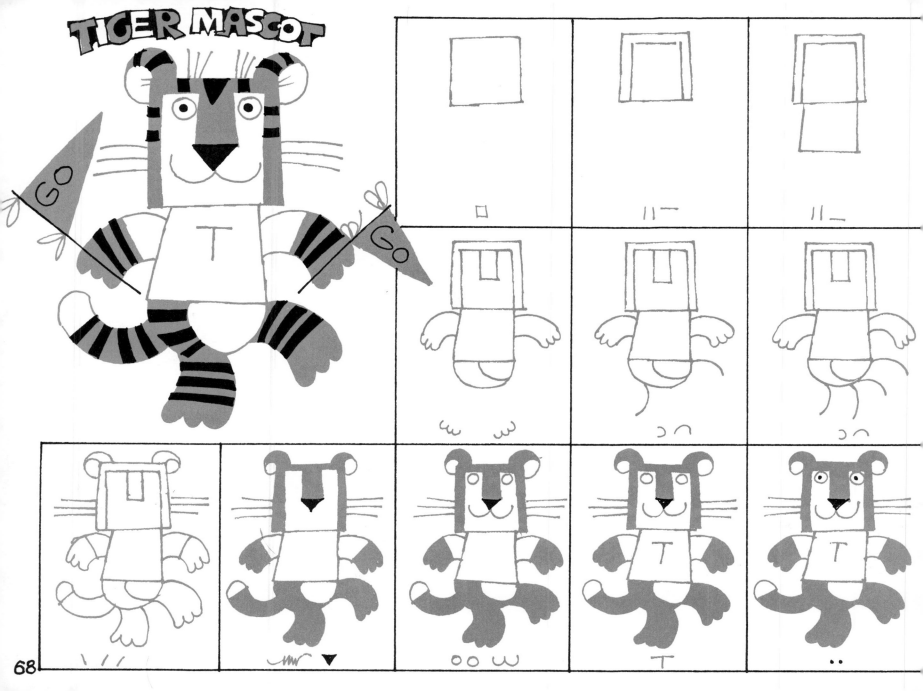

TIGER MASCOT

68

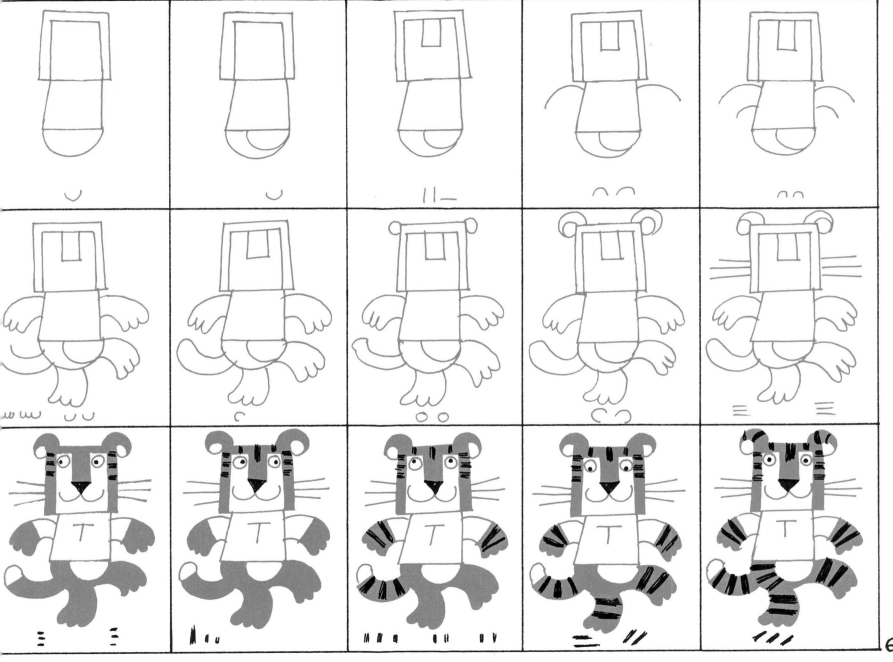

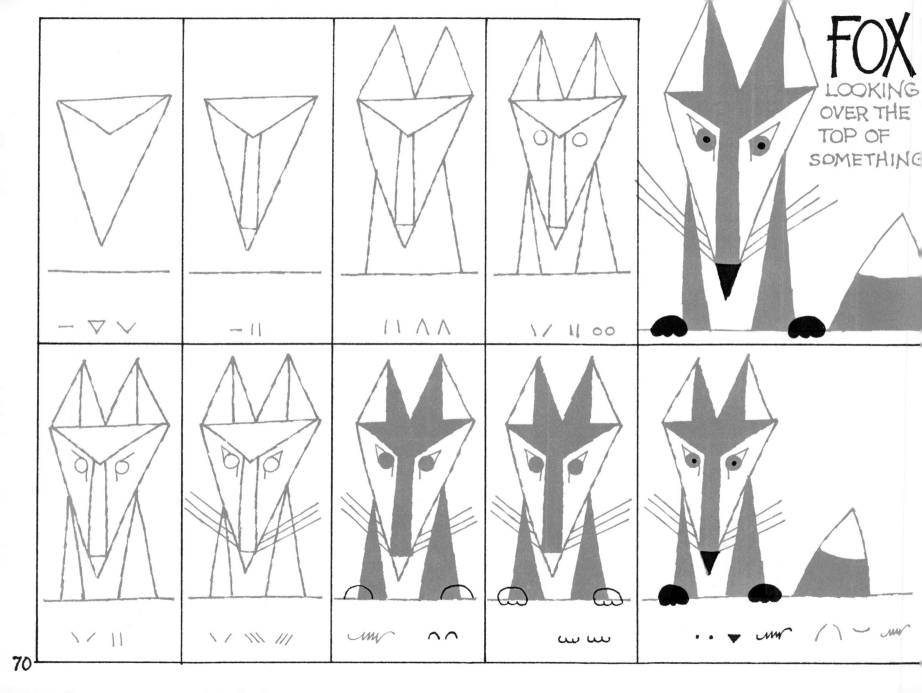

FOX

LOOKING
OVER THE
TOP OF
SOMETHING

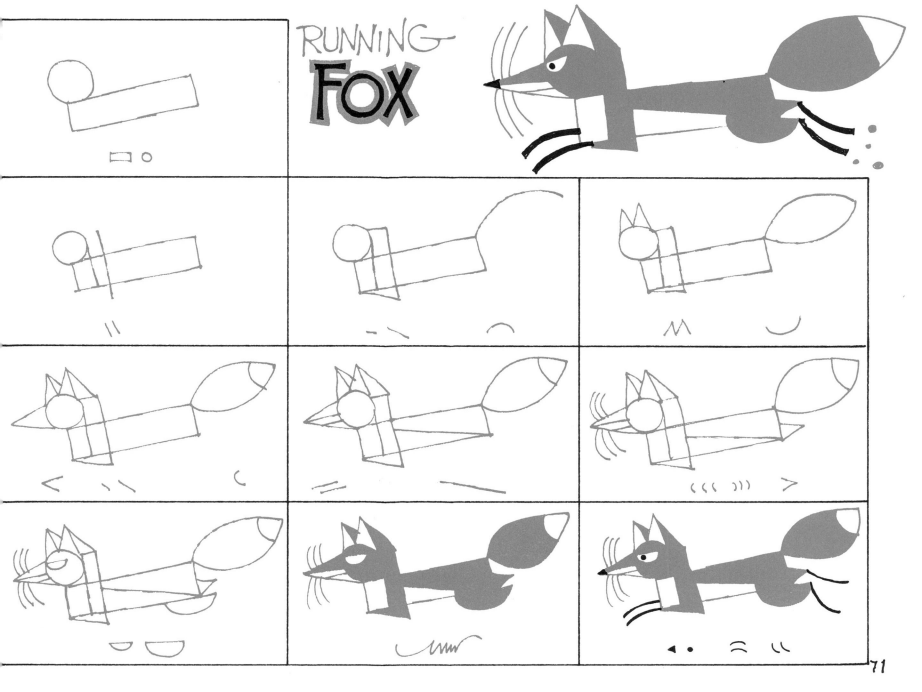

RUNNING FOX

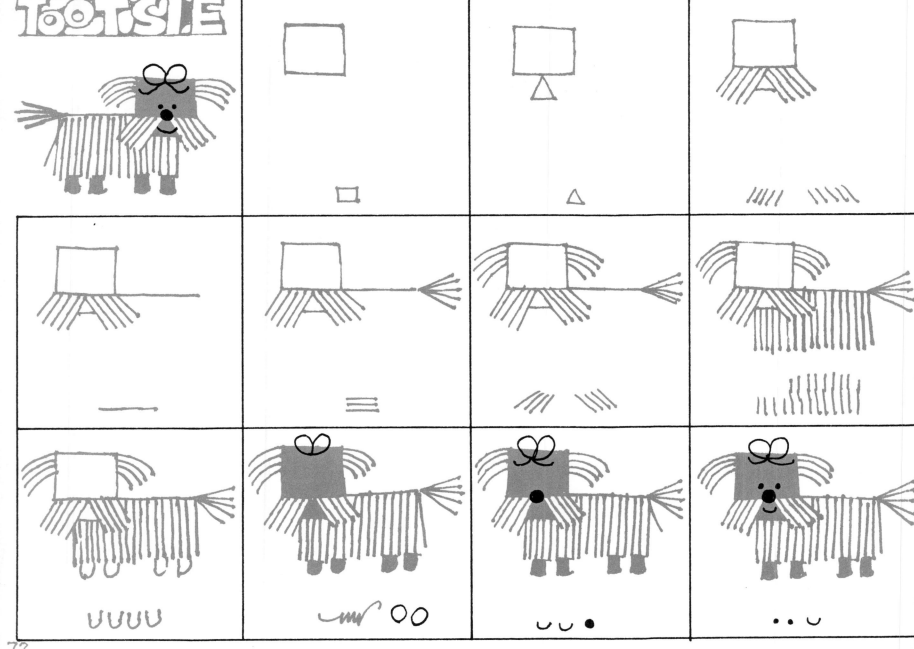

TOOTSIE

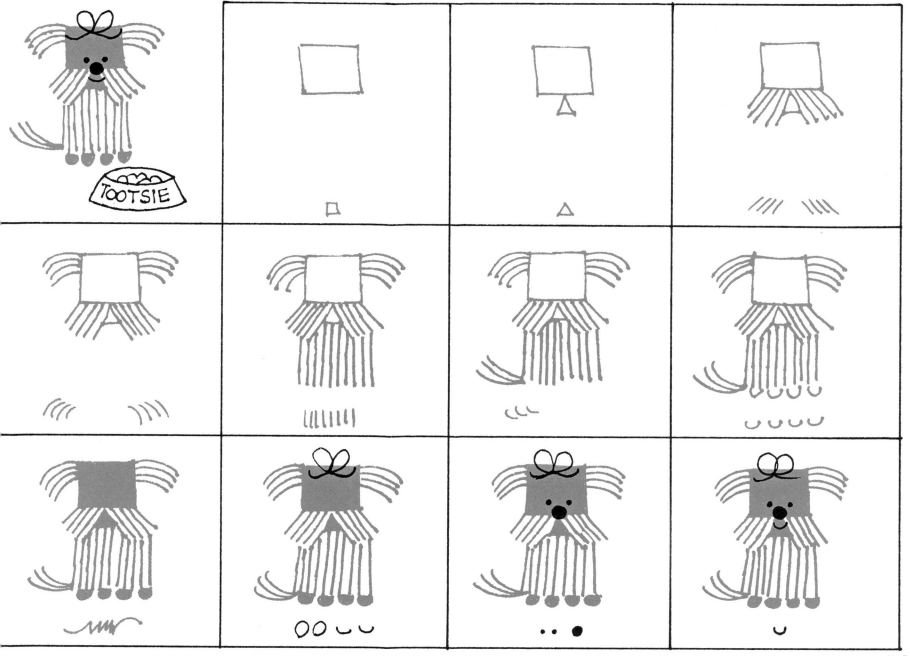

WILLUM

\\ //

ᴄᴜ ᴄᴜ ᴄᴜ ᴄᴜ

∧ ∧

▸▾◂

∵ ∴

ETC.

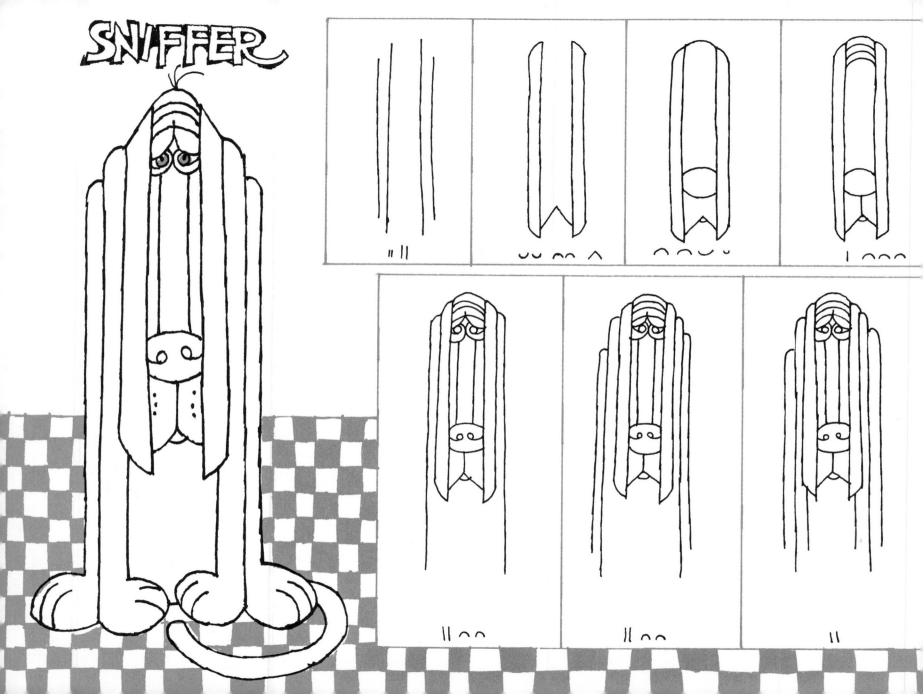

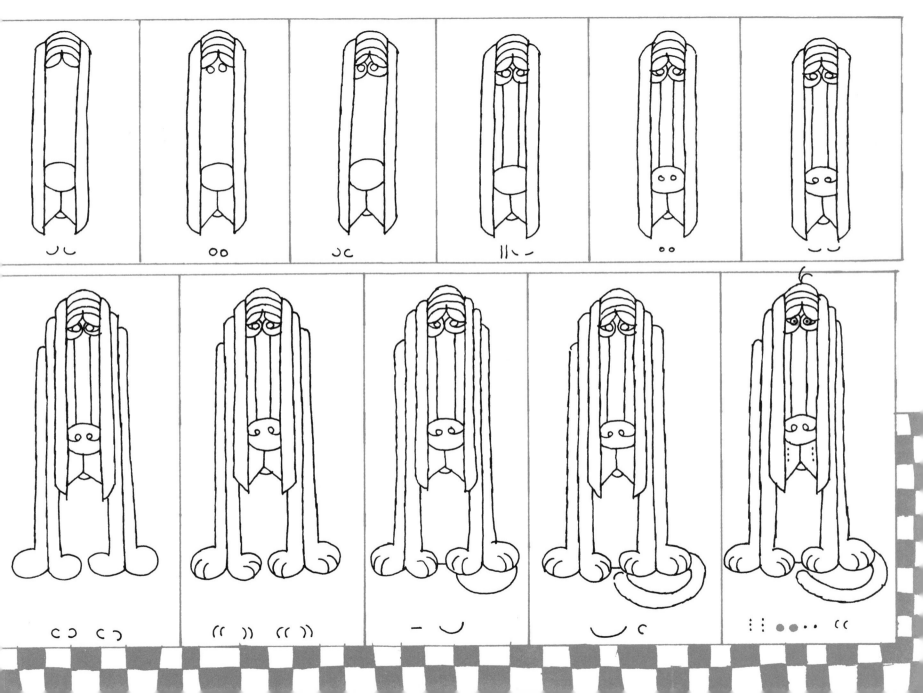

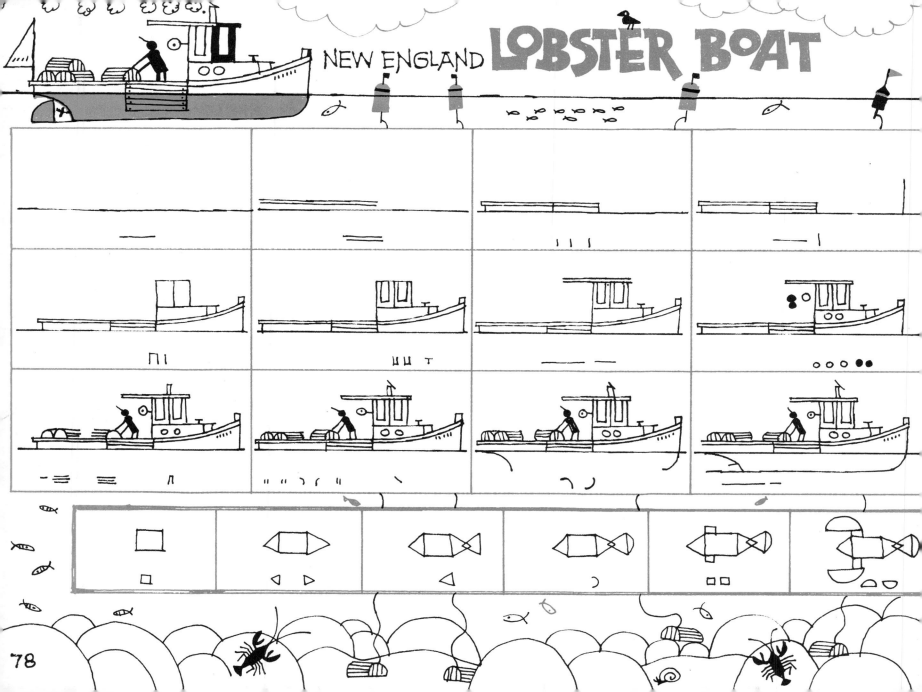

NEW ENGLAND **LOBSTER BOAT**

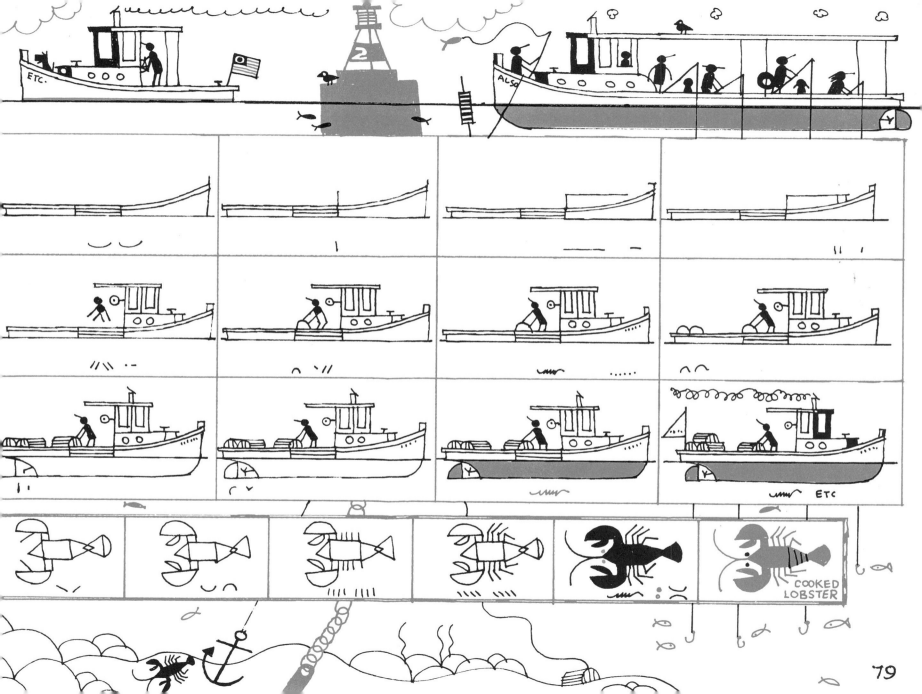

ETC.

ALSO

COOKED
LOBSTER

ETC

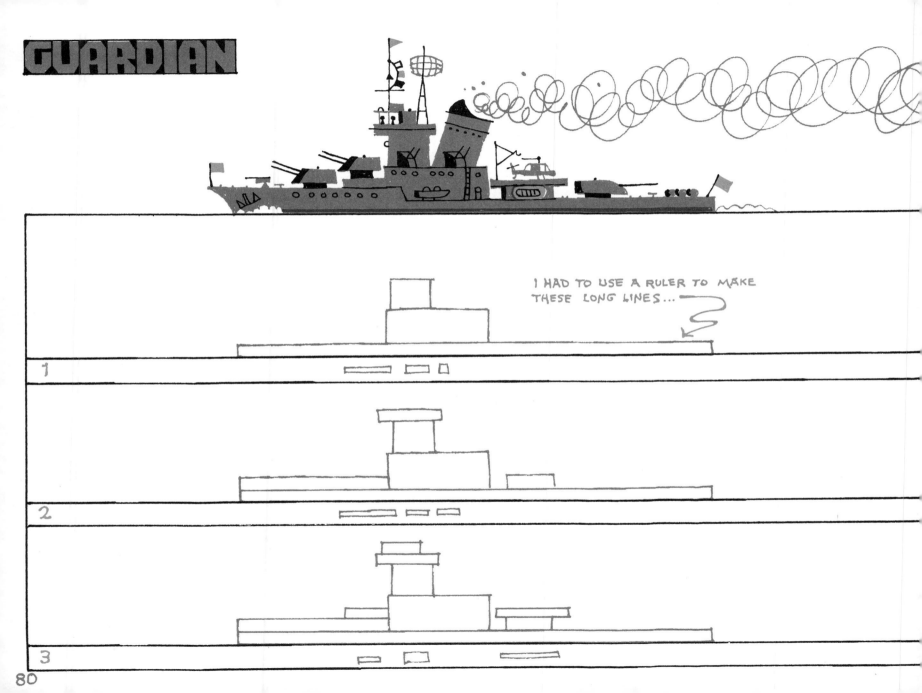

GUARDIAN

I HAD TO USE A RULER TO MAKE THESE LONG LINES...

1

2

3

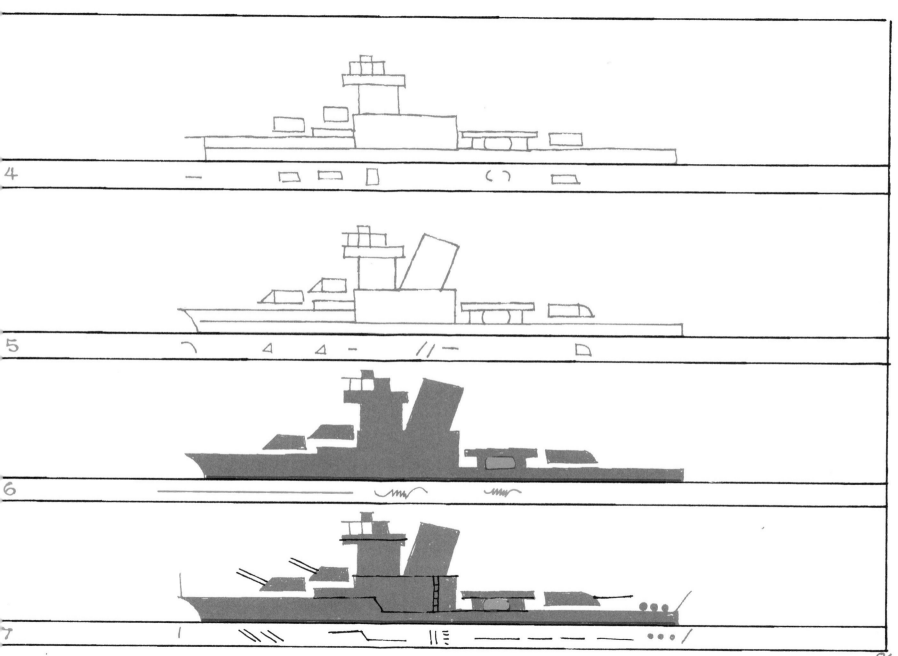

4

5

6

7

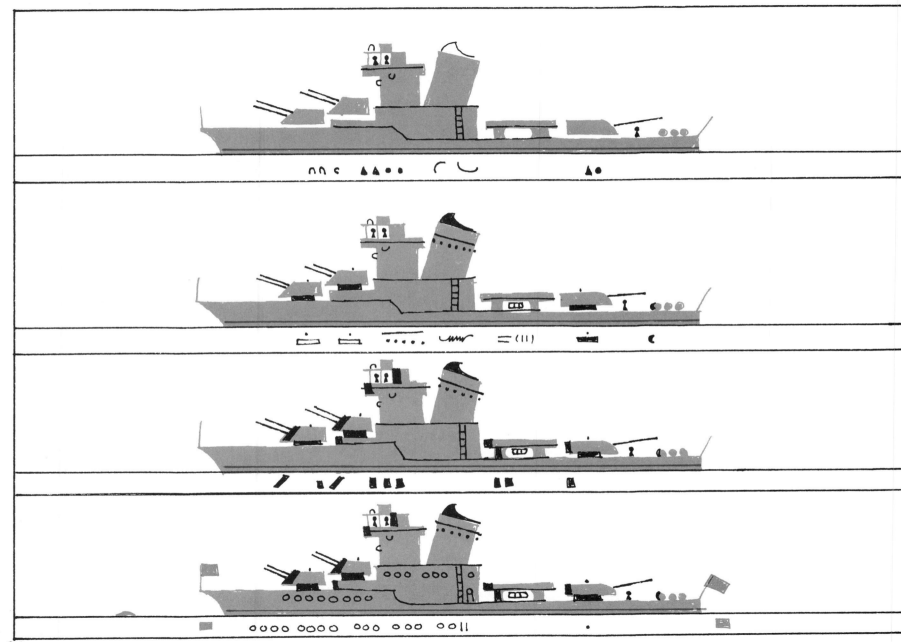

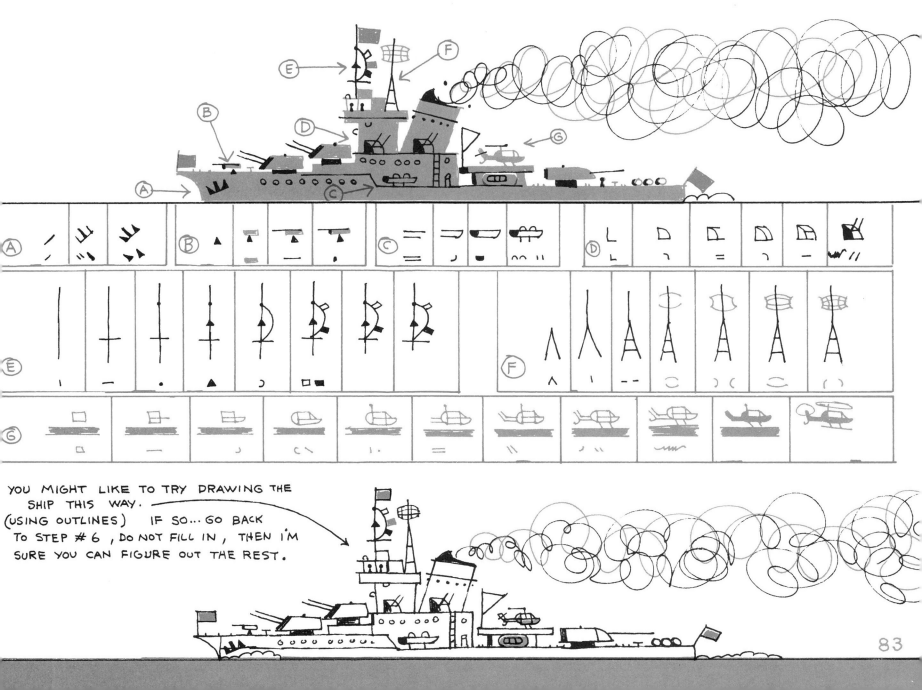

YOU MIGHT LIKE TO TRY DRAWING THE SHIP THIS WAY.
(USING OUTLINES) IF SO... GO BACK TO STEP #6, DO NOT FILL IN, THEN I'M SURE YOU CAN FIGURE OUT THE REST.

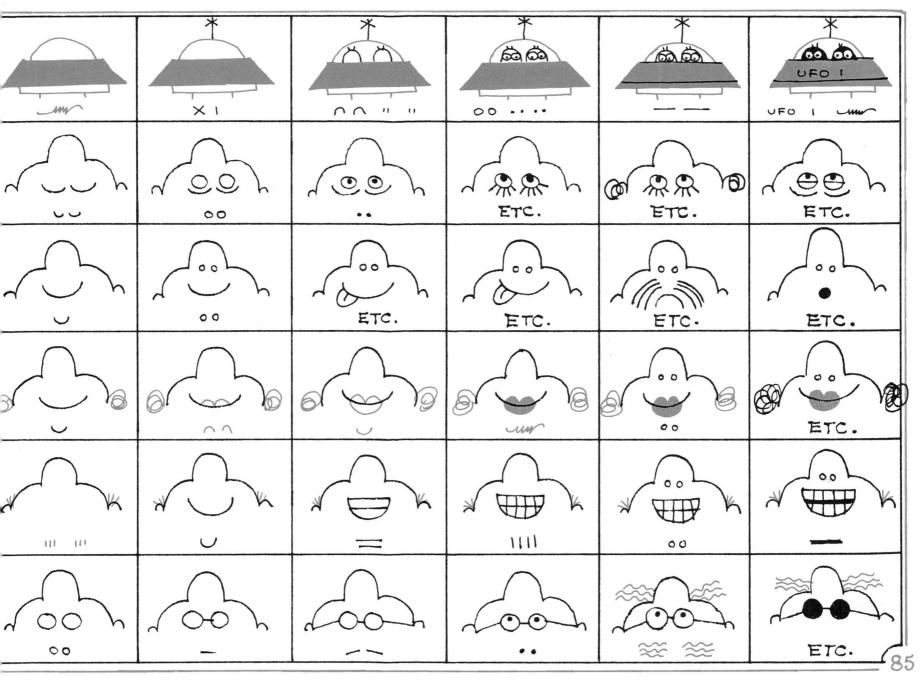

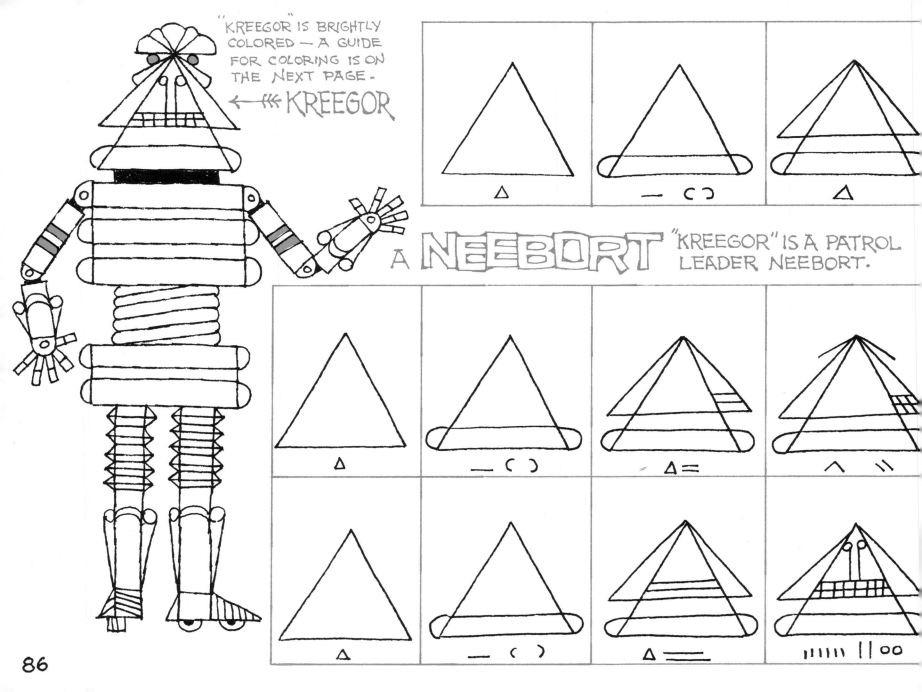

"KREEGOR" IS BRIGHTLY
COLORED — A GUIDE
FOR COLORING IS ON
THE NEXT PAGE.
← ⟨⟨⟨ KREEGOR

A NEEBORT   "KREEGOR" IS A PATROL
LEADER NEEBORT.

△

— ⊂⊃

△

△

— ⊂ ⊃

△ =

⌒ \\

△

— ⊂ ⊃

△ =

|||||| | | ∞

86

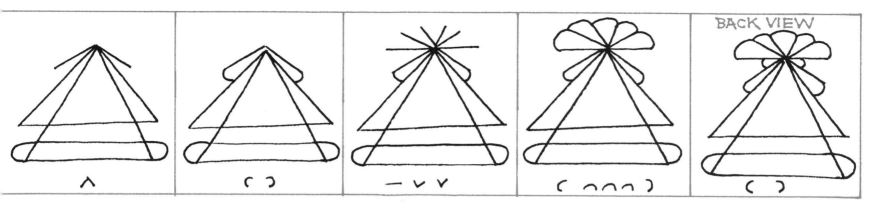

PATROL LEADER NEEBORTS SUCH AS "KREEGOR" TELL FROOS AND DRIMS WHAT TO DO.
(FROOS & DRIMS ARE IN THE BIG PURPLE DRAWING BOOK.)

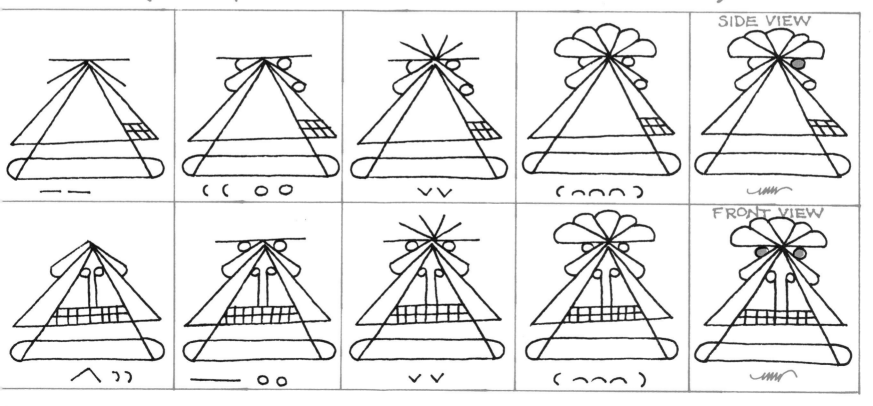

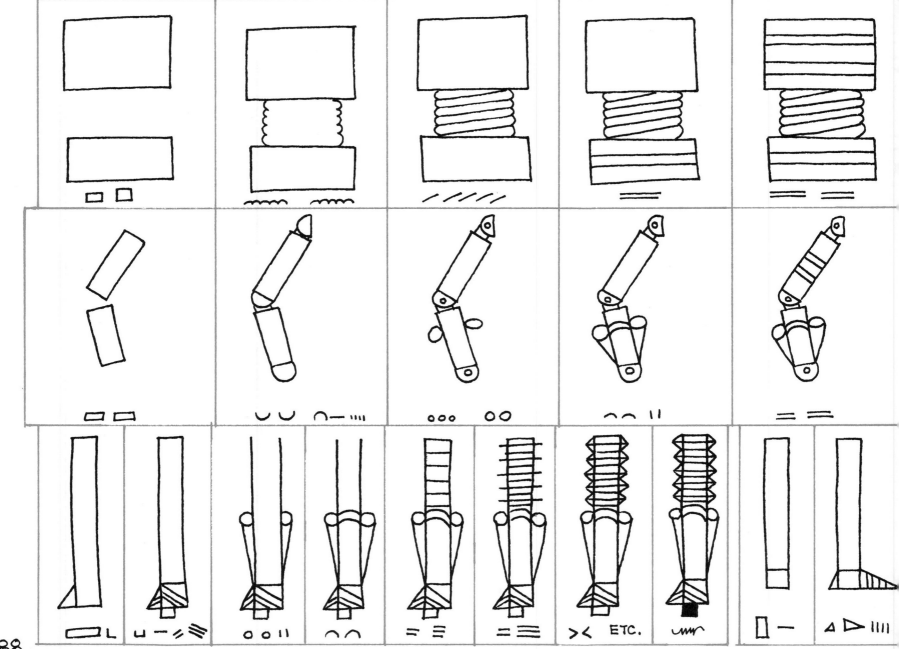

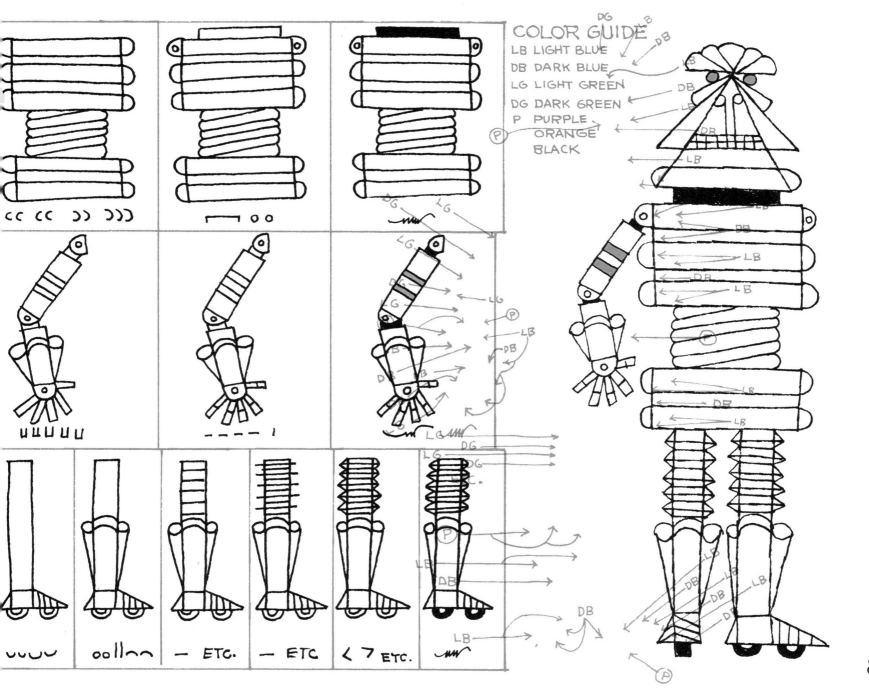

COLOR GUIDE
LB LIGHT BLUE
DB DARK BLUE
LG LIGHT GREEN
DG DARK GREEN
P PURPLE
ORANGE
BLACK

89

ERTS ARE FOUND NEAR THE PLANET ZORT.*
HOME PLANET UNKNOWN. THEY ARE DESCRIBED AS BEING SMALL,
CURIOUS, SHY, AND ORANGE. THEIR SPACECRAFT ARE CAPABLE OF
BURSTS OF INCREDIBLE SPEED. THIS FACT COMBINED WITH THEIR
SHYNESS RESULTS IN VERY LITTLE BEING KNOWN ABOUT THEM.
WHAT LITTLE IS KNOWN IS PRESENTED HERE. PERHAPS MORE
WILL BE DISCOVERED BY SOME ENTERPRISING YOUNG ARTIST.

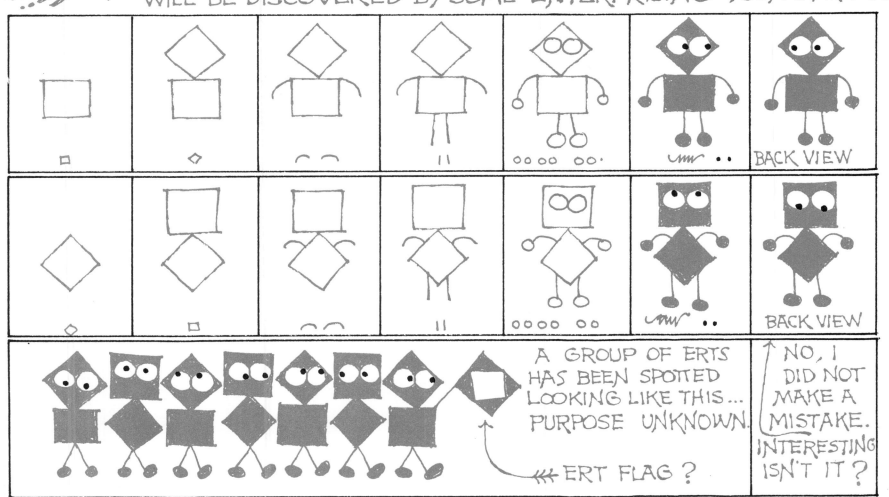

BACK VIEW

BACK VIEW

A GROUP OF ERTS
HAS BEEN SPOTTED
LOOKING LIKE THIS...
PURPOSE UNKNOWN.

← ERT FLAG ?

NO, I
DID NOT
MAKE A
MISTAKE.
INTERESTING
ISN'T IT ?

90

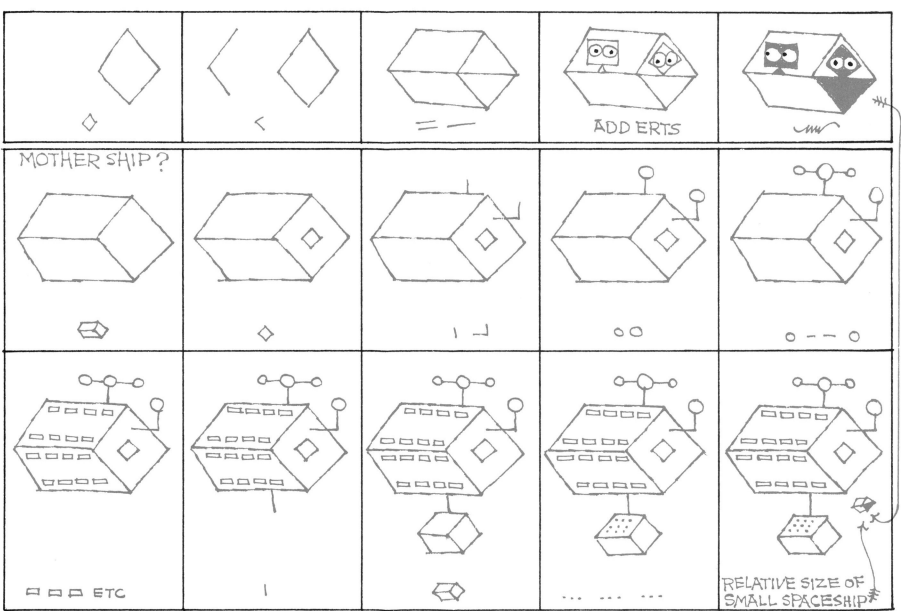

ADD ERTS

MOTHER SHIP?

□ □ □ ETC

RELATIVE SIZE OF
SMALL SPACESHIP*

CONTENTS

OTHER EMBERLEY DRAWING BOOKS:

ED EMBERLEY'S DRAWING BOOK OF ANIMALS
" " " FACES
" " " MAKE A WORLD
" " GREAT THUMBPRINT DRAWING BOOK
" " BIG GREEN DRAWING BOOK
" " BIG PURPLE DRAWING BOOK ← COMING SOON !

ED EMBERLEY'S LITTLE DRAWING BOOK OF BIRDS
" " " " TRAINS
" " " " WEIRDOS
" " " " THE FARM

★ ALSO DINOSAURS, A DRAWING BOOK BY MICHAEL EMBERLEY

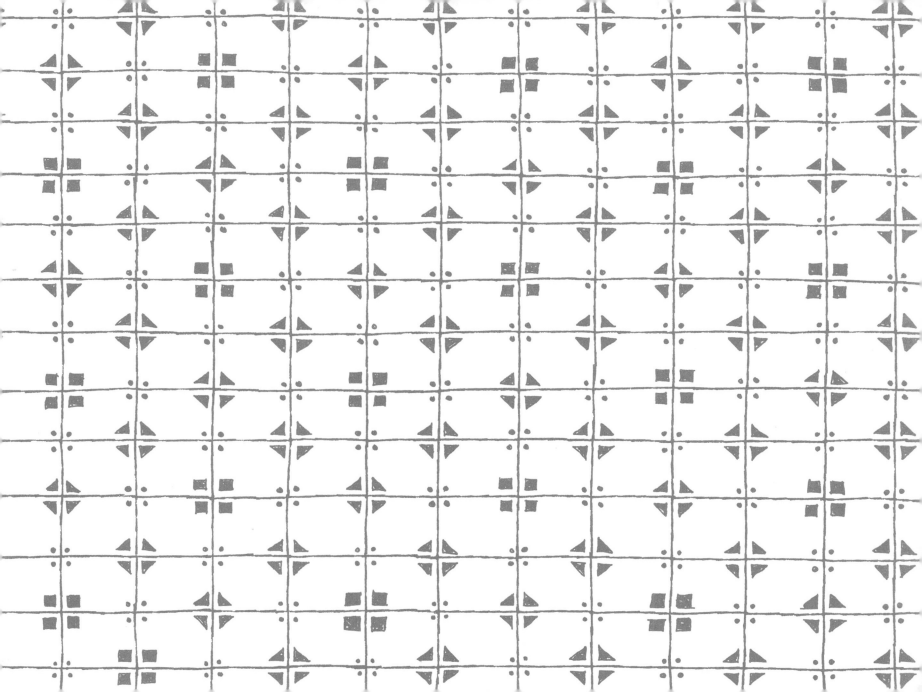